M000307918

CORE
CONFIDENCE

CORE CONFIDENCE

OWN YOUR TALENT • FACE YOUR FEAR
CREATE YOUR FUTURE

KATE BOORER AND FIONA PEARMAN

www.coreconfidence.com.au

This is a work of nonfiction. Nonetheless, some of the names and personal characteristics of the individuals or events involved have been changed in order to disguise their identities. Any resulting resemblance to persons living or dead is entirely coincidental and unintentional.

First published in 2018 in Australia

Copyright © Kate Boorer and Fiona Pearman 2018

All rights reserved. Except as permitted under the *Australian Copyright Act 1968* (for example, a fair dealing for the purposes of study, research, criticism or review), no part of this book may be reproduced, stored in a retrieval system, communicated or transmitted in any form or by any means without prior permission in writing from the authors. All inquiries should be made to the authors.

All efforts were taken to acknowledge reference material reproduced in this book. The authors welcome information in this regard.

ISBN: 978-0-6483551-1-3 (paperback)

 NATIONAL LIBRARY OF AUSTRALIA

A catalogue record for this book is available from the National Library of Australia

Edited by Jules Stopp
Cover design Michelle Sargent

Kate Boorer and Fiona Pearman are available as consultants and keynote speakers on the subject of confidence. For further information, visit www.coreconfidence.com.au

For working women everywhere

CONTENTS

The act of *confidence* comes before the feeling of *confidence*[1]

INTRODUCTION

We have been in the business of empowering professionals – from established leaders to emerging talent – for many years. In that time, we have become aware through our coaching practice, corporate leadership programs, conferences and workshops of an alarming trend among the women we've met, and continue to meet - a lack of sustainable confidence.

Our research tells us that most women will experience a crisis of confidence at some point in their career, regardless of what they do, who they work with or how highly they are regarded.

When we ask our clients to define what confidence is however, neither men nor women find it easy to quantify. The people we work with usually list a series of qualities they associate with confidence to describe it, or they point to the most confident person in the room to show what confidence looks like. Given confidence is a performance measure in most companies – and women receive a lot of feedback in this area – it's concerning that a working definition is not universally agreed or understood.

While as a society we believe in the concept of fairness and equality, and raise our children upon these pillars, many workplaces have a long way to go to demonstrate equality in action. Gender balance at senior levels is still an issue. Combined with the undermining of women's confidence from an early age, is it any wonder women are left wondering "am I good enough?"

We have now spent over a decade working with a variety of modalities, programs, coaching techniques and experts to unpack the beliefs and behaviours that limit forward movement in business and life at large.

This journey has been driven by a passionate fascination with personal development and the research and resources available to help people tap into their truth and power. While many esteemed books and authors (who we admire) line our shelves, few if any provide a step-by-step guide to uncovering Core Confidence.

Which leads us to this book and you.

The beginnings of the book started many years ago as an experiential Confidence Workshop (that continues to run to this day). We wanted to explore the confidence deficit we were encountering and enable women to:

- Connect or reconnect with their inner strength and power

- Design their lives mindfully and purposefully

- Have the courage to ask for what they want and deserve

Through our work, we have witnessed thousands of women making profound and courageous decisions for their future; transforming their lives by asking themselves the right questions at the right time. These women have proved that even when Core Confidence is neglected, it is never too late to listen in and take positive action.

Now, we want to share the **"How-To"** of Core Confidence on a larger stage for the benefit of women everywhere.

The goal of Core Confidence is to challenge you to take ownership of your talents and put them in the service of your best and most daring self, not only for your own advancement but to act as a strong role model for those girls and women behind and beside you. Creating new rules for yourself and the environment you work within requires curiosity, experimentation and courage, and that's where we come in.

In this book we will provide you with:

- A working definition of Core Confidence

- Ten dimensions (internal and external) - the building blocks to a confident self

- The practices and coaching that will reconnect you with unshakeable unbreakable Core Confidence

- Insight into the systemic, gender and personal barriers to confidence

- Suggestions for how to use your confidence to advocate for others

We will also share stories of the women we've met who have bravely faced their fears and developed or rediscovered their Core Confidence and explore why your network is one of your biggest professional and personal assets.

We are grateful to have learnt from some of the most talented and inspiring people and teachers throughout the years. Core Confidence is a tribute to our network and most importantly the women who have inspired and encouraged us to bring this work to life.

The book is divided into three sections. In Section One we explore why the conversation around confidence is so important, personal confidence barriers and lay out our definition of Core Confidence. Section Two contains the ten building blocks of Core Confidence and includes practical exercises designed to help you integrate the information on a deep, personal level. Finally, in Section Three we unpack the role of advocacy to create sustainable change that addresses the systemic, gender and practical barriers that women continue to face in the workplace.

As you read through the book you will notice we've included our stories and those of clients and colleagues. When sharing our own stories we identify whether it's Kate or Fiona's story by putting our name in brackets after the first 'I'. We've used the same conversational language we do in our workshops, which means at times we use 'we' to refer to us as authors, women and collectively with you the reader. We also speak directly to you as the reader inviting your participation in reconnecting with your Core Confidence.

Now, it' all about you. We are thrilled to take this journey by your side.

Kate & Fiona

SECTION

ONE

THE ILLUSION DELUSION

Whenever you set off on a new path, it's important to know where you're headed, the terrain in front of you and the types of obstacles you might encounter along the way. The road to confidence is no different.

In this Section, we begin the conversation about the current social, political and organisational landscape (with a full discussion in Section Three), explore the unique barriers to women's progression and clearly define Core Confidence.

THE LANDSCAPE

"When I first entered the workforce, in 1991, there were just as many women as men going into entry-level jobs. I looked to the side of me, and it was equal. But I looked above me, and it was almost entirely men. As my career progressed, I had fewer and fewer women in every group I was part of. If you look back at the 1950s, '60s, or '70s, of course we've made progress. But we have not made progress in getting a greater share of the top jobs, in any industry, in the past decade."

- Sheryl Sandberg

Let's set the scene.

There is a casual assumption that the battle for women's liberation has been won – that the glass ceiling has been smashed at all seniority levels, equitable pay is mandated and the ability to both raise a family and progress your career is institutionalised. It follows then that *feminism* has no place in this new world and is simply an outdated ideology pushed by angry women.

The research however, provides a stark contrast to these assumptions. So stark in fact, we experienced a sense of unease when reading the latest reports about women's so-called liberation. The statistics for women in leadership, women's economic outcomes (pay and super) and support for working parents are shocking. Surely, we couldn't still have so far to go?

While most children are raised with the same rights and opportunities irrespective of gender, by the time boys and girls become men and women in the workforce their rights, opportunities and outcomes look very different:

- In Australia women represent 47%[2] of graduates; by the time they reach senior management level they represent 35% of senior managers but by the time they reach executive levels, they only account for 16% of CEOs[3] and only 5% of ASX 200 CEOs[4].

- The gender pay gap has remained relatively steady, hovering between 15% and 19% over the past 20 years[5]. In fact, based on the 2017 Global Gender Gap[6] Report by the World Economic Forum, it will take another 217 years to close the economic gender gap.

- Only one in four mothers with children under the age of 5 works full time[7].

Some of the most compelling data comes from the most recent *Workplace Gender Equality Agency*[8] (WGEA) report, representing 4 million employees, 11,000 employers and 40% of employees in Australia (of which 50% are female). Their 2017 report shows limited progress for women in management over the last four years:

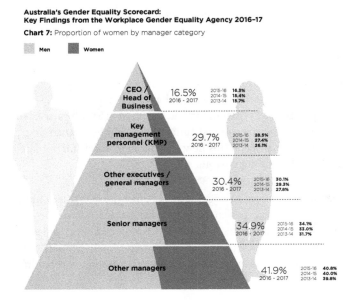

Australia's Gender Equality Scorecard:
Key Findings from the Workplace Gender Equality Agency 2016–17

Chart 7: Proportion of women by manager category

Men   Women

| CEO / Head of Business | 16.5% 2016 - 2017 | 2015-16 16.3% / 2014-15 15.4% / 2013-14 15.7% |

| Key management personnel (KMP) | 29.7% 2016 - 2017 | 2015-16 28.5% / 2014-15 27.4% / 2013-14 26.1% |

| Other executives / general managers | 30.4% 2016 - 2017 | 2015-16 30.1% / 2014-15 29.3% / 2013-14 27.8% |

| Senior managers | 34.9% 2016 - 2017 | 2015-16 34.1% / 2014-15 33.0% / 2013-14 31.7% |

| Other managers | 41.9% 2016 - 2017 | 2015-16 40.8% / 2014-15 40.0% / 2013-14 39.8% |

In this landscape, women remain significantly underrepresented at the highest levels of power and decision making across all areas of society, government and business.

THE BARRIERS

We have met many women who despite being seen by others as confident and having it all together, share within the safety of a coaching conversation or workshop their truth: "inside I don't feel confident at all". These women have convinced themselves that they are the problem, however we know that a multitude of factors are at play.

Many of the barriers to self belief and self agency sit outside of your immediate control. This is good news. When women are clear about the landscape, they can determine the skills, capabilities and attributes they need to rise to the challenge.

We have categorised the *barriers to confidence* into four core areas. Some are part of a complex interplay of societal expectations and bias, while others are practical and structural issues which limit women's progression in the workplace. It might be time to change the question from "What's wrong with me?" to "What's wrong with the system?"

The four barriers

1. *Systemic barriers*
The subtle and long-held views that cause society to treat girls differently and structure careers and parenthood in a way that challenges women

2. *Gender bias barriers*
Those specific, well documented ways in which gender bias effectively limits career progression for women

3. *Practical barriers*
The entrenched traditional model of full-time male breadwinner is hard to disrupt when there is little support and incentive to do so

4. *Personal confidence barriers*

The way in which women consciously and unconsciously limit themselves

The first three barriers are explored in more detail in Section Three. There, we'll show you how your confidence journey can impact the future of women. For now, let's focus on the personal confidence barriers.

Let's get personal

Our job is to shine a light on the complexity of this issue, unpack the dynamics of your relationship with confidence and show you the areas where you have ownership and opportunity to reconnect with your confident self. As you read, get curious about whether any of these barriers are familiar to you:

52%

of the 2000 women surveyed by Women's Agenda for their 2017 Ambition Report said confidence in their abilities could hinder their ambitions

Self sabotage through perfectionism

We can be our own worst enemies. Many women end up pursuing perfectionism in their career believing that by working hard and learning all there is to know, confidence and progression will be the natural outcomes. Along the way, these women have failed to understand that in most careers this won't get you to the top of your field. In fact, perfectionism sets such an unrealistic goal that it sabotages our efforts.

If this is you, you'll be familiar with:

- Investing too many hours to stay on top of issues and information for fear of being asked a question you can't answer

- Not speaking up in a meeting for fear of getting it wrong and how this might impact on your reputation

- Compromising everything personally to prove your value or worse, cross every 'i' and dot every 't' so that failure is prevented no matter what the cost

Self doubt

In our experience, women are likely to apply for a job only when they feel they meet 100% of the criteria listed, while men are more likely to apply for jobs when they think they have 60% of the criteria.

We have learned that women – on the whole – underestimate their abilities, downplay their strengths and want to be 120% sure they are able to do something well before they put their hand up. In 2011, the Institute of Leadership and Management in the United Kingdom surveyed British managers about how confident they felt in their professions. Half the female respondents reported self doubt compared with fewer than a third of male respondents[9]. In another study published in 2011, Ernesto Reuben, a professor at Columbia Business School, found that men consistently rated their past performance about 30% higher than it actually was[10].

Being invisible

Young girls are socialised to be good and not make a noise, mess or fuss. Unfortunately, for women, that no fuss attitude can make it difficult for others to see you, and therein lies the problem. A study in 2012 by researchers from Brigham Young University and Princeton found that, when a mixed group collaborates to solve a problem, men will take up 75% of the conversation[11]. If women don't learn how to or fail to speak up, we can guarantee they cannot be heard or seen. Learning how to find your voice and hold your ground are critical skills that influence how others think about you and what you're trying to say.

Lack of self acknowledgement

Women tend to have an inclusive and collaborative perspective; they will often promote the achievements of the whole team and readily praise the performance of others. A 2013 study by Michelle Haynes and Madeleine Heilman, found that when men and women were assigned to work on a project together, women gave more credit to their male teammates and took less credit for themselves[12]. While this approach fosters team spirit and performance, it can mean that women fail to acknowledge their personal achievements, impacting how they are seen in the organisation (their personal brand), something that men tend to do more naturally.

Whether you *think* you can or you can't, you're *right*

- Henry Ford

Maybe women think it is egotistical to *self promote* or *big note* themselves and many highly successful women have attributed their success to luck and being in the right place at the right time. A 2011 study by UK based think tank Catalyst[13] found that of all the career advancement strategies used by women, making their achievements known was the only one associated with remuneration growth.

While acknowledging your achievements might not come easily to you, there are ways to do it that do not require an overinflated ego, as we will discuss in later chapters.

Not asking for what you want

When coaching men and women to negotiate salary, it is surprising how often women shy away from asking for what they are worth. They are less likely to negotiate salary (either when taking on new roles or as part of the annual review process) and are more likely to accept what is first offered. Linda Babcock, a professor of economics at Carnegie Mellon University and the author of *Women Don't Ask[14]*, found in studies of business-school students, that men initiate salary negotiations four times as often as women do, and that when women do negotiate, they ask for and get – on average, 30% less money than men.

We see these barriers play out regularly in the workplace: holding your tongue in critical moments when your voice could make the difference, hiding your skills, talents and insights and reaping fewer rewards than you deserve.

IT'S TIME TO RISE

The landscape we find ourselves operating in poses unique and interesting challenges that need to be met by strong and confident women. The conversation now is **how**. How do we get you thinking, feeling and doing things differently?

We continually hear our workshop participants say things like, "I have been told I have the capability to progress, but need to work on building my confidence", or "I wanted the opportunity but wasn't confident enough to go for it". Many clients ask us how to develop confidence or tell us that their confidence has taken a beating and they don't know what to do.

These comments are all too common for women in Australian organisations. In 2017 a study by Chief Executive Women and Bain[15] found that women are twice as likely as men to be told that they need to display "more confidence" and that women are less likely than men to receive clear feedback on what they need to do to be ready for promotion. The lack of actionable feedback for women trying to progress their careers was one of the things that drew us to investigating the notion of confidence and how it plays out for women and men.

WHAT IS CONFIDENCE?

Despite this new focus on women and confidence in the workplace, the definition of confidence still remains somewhat vague. What are these talented women lacking exactly? Is it a quality? A skill? An energy? All of the above or something else?

As it stands, the most common definitions of confidence are:

• Confidence is the feeling or belief that one can have faith in or rely on someone or something

• Confidence is the state of feeling certain about the truth of something

• Confidence is a feeling of self assurance arising from an appreciation of our own abilities or qualities, and acknowledgment of our current limits

• Confidence is risking failure, knowing you will be ok

• Confidence is turning thoughts and decisions into action

While each of these aspects are important, they don't encapsulate all that we know to be the felt sense of confidence. And given the ambiguity, how is anyone ever held accountable for getting it wrong?

Our proposition
is that *Core
Confidence* is
within you and our
job is to reconnect
you to it

I'VE GOT THIS (AND SO HAVE YOU)

We break our confidence definition into three distinctive parts:

1. *The working definition of confidence*
The mantra you need to bring confidence to mind effortlessly in any situation.

2. *The expression of confidence*
What confidence looks and feels like to you and those around you (the measurable aspect of confidence).

3. *The building blocks of confidence*
The 10 dimensions of confidence and the tools and strategies to leverage them.

CORE CONFIDENCE MANTRA IS QUITE SIMPLY **"I'VE GOT THIS"**

Sarah, a client of ours, changed organisations after nearly 10 years with her old company. It was a risk, but she was ready. Sarah told us that for the first time in her career she turned up on Day One with excitement rather than fear. When we asked what was different now, she said "It's a mindset. I knew I had this". What Sarah understood about herself was that no matter what challenge she faced, she would be ok. She knew she had the skills and experience to learn quickly, adapt and figure out the elements of the role. She wasn't afraid of mistakes and looked forward to sharing what she already knew. But, more than that, she trusted herself. If the organisation turned out to be the wrong fit, she would make a different decision. Sarah couldn't lose.

While it may be fleeting for some of us, we all know that feeling. The feeling of being in flow, knowing what we stand for, connecting with others in a productive manner and managing challenges with positivity. When we are excited about what we'll learn and how we'll grow, rather than weighed down by our perceived flaws or lack of knowledge.

Think about the last time you stood in your power and said "I've got this". What's getting in the way of you experiencing it, right now?

Core Confidence expressed

"I've got this" is shorthand for *I have the physical, emotional, spiritual and intellectual capacity to meet the task or situation in front of me*. It is an internal alignment visible to others through our actions, energy, body language and speech. It is an essence rather than a *thing* and when it is expressed in the world it is unmistakable:

- *Taking action* – moving forward and doing

- *Being decisive* – free of doubt, no second-guessing or approval seeking

- *Self belief* – having faith in who you are and backing it

- *Resilience* – navigating failure and difficulty with humility

- *Self honesty* – acknowledging the truth even when it is hard

- *Authentic energy* – a total absence of pretending

- *Awareness* – understanding self in relation to others and the environment

- *Curiosity* – the ability to learn rather than know

It takes our workshop participants no time at all to pinpoint where they shine and what they shy away from. They feel for the first time they can name specifically the areas where confidence is absent for them.

When leaders give the feedback that you need more confidence, they are highlighting an area of confidence they can't see in you. Using the expressions of confidence provides the language to delve deeper with your leaders and ask, "which characteristic of confidence is currently not being demonstrated?".

Core Confidence - The building blocks

In Section Two we have identified ten interwoven dimensions of Core Confidence. It is not our intention or belief that Core Confidence only exists when you have nailed them all; they are simply elements that when activated can help reconnect you with what we know is already present.....your Core Confidence. The first five factors may be somewhat familiar, as they cover the traditional subjects of leadership theory and training:

External elements of confidence, those aspects focused on **what you are doing**

- Get Clear (Chapter 1)
- Set Goals and Take Action (Chapter 2)
- Know Your Stuff (Chapter 3)
- Work Hard (Chapter 4)
- Build Relationships (Chapter 5)

While these elements are crucial, on their own they can be a fragile foundation that when challenged can come falling down like a pack of cards. To be able to trust yourself in new and challenging situations, you'll need to know who you are beyond your goals and subject matter expertise. Core Confidence is an inner game.

Internal elements of confidence, those aspects focused on **who you are being**

- Be Focused and Present (Chapter 6)
- Maintain Resilience (Chapter 7)
- Be Authentic (Chapter 8)
- Ask for Help (Chapter 9)
- Face Fear (Chapter 10)

As you work through the book, we can't promise you immediate change and unassailable self belief. But, we can promise that you will develop:

- Awareness and clarity about what true confidence is

- A map to understand what is going on for you and your relationship with confidence in any moment

- The tools and strategies to get yourself back on track

Confidence is a self-fulfilling prophecy; the more you connect with the ten dimensions of confidence the more you will reinforce your sense of self. For those who choose self-doubt, the only outcome is more of the same.

It's time to move beyond wondering why and take control of the how. How you, personally, get to your *I've got this* moment.

Core Confidence is when, at in the deepest part of your soul, you believe in who you are, the value you contribute and the person you are becoming. Simply put, it is the ability to know "I've got this" and be unshakeable in your resolve

SECTION
TWO

SECTION

TWO

THE BUILDING BLOCKS

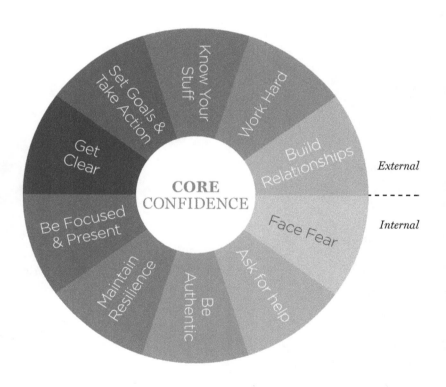

Chapter 1

GET CLEAR

If confidence
is in part defined
*by honesty
with yourself,*
then get honest
about what you
value

In our practice, we are often asked, "What is the most important attribute needed to access confidence?", and the simple answer is *clarity*. Becoming clear about your professional and personal values is a crucial first step on the confidence journey and is inextricably linked to the ability to make sound decisions.

Think about what it *feels* or looks like when you are unclear of what you really want. When you can't name or explain where you're headed. Making a decision about the next stage of your career seems impossible and you zig-zag between options with little or no confidence about which direction to take. When a decision is finally made, relief is simply overridden by a barrage of *what ifs*?

Compare this with someone who is clear about their values; someone who knows precisely what is important to them in the context of their career and life. This person can readily articulate the type of work environment that inspires them, find alignment between their personal and organisational values and share their career aspirations openly.

When important decisions need to be made, they assess the options against their values and goals, and use this framework to make informed choices in areas such as career planning and progression, family, health and personal development.

This does not mean that decisions in this context are neatly packaged or without compromise. On the contrary, a person with clarity makes real choices with both conviction and acceptance; acknowledging what they are choosing, why they are choosing it and what they are saying no to, in order to achieve those goals.

CLARITY REQUIRES BEING PREPARED TO LET GO OF OPTIONS THAT ARE RECOGNISED AS LESS IMPORTANT

Understanding *what matters most to you* is a process that cannot be overlooked as you reconnect with your Core Confidence.

WHO IS DRIVING?
KATE'S PERSONAL STORY

At the tender age of 18, I (Kate) decided to pursue a career in business and finance. Far from the cardigan wearing stereotype, I could see my future self in a large corner office with full glass windows, wearing a power suit and a stylish French roll (for those not familiar with 90's power dressing, that's a hairstyle not a food). With my vision in mind, I was ready to do this thing we call growing up.

Fast forward 10 years – after diligent study, long hours and fierce ambition – I achieved my goal. I was an executive in a respected organisation, with a six figure salary, living in a dream suburb. I had made it to the *destination of success* where the experience of fulfillment was promised to await and I had arrived earlier than expected.

But, fulfillment never arrived. Rather than basking in achievement, I was deeply unsettled, uninspired and bored. Why wasn't society's roadmap for success producing any type of contentment? This was a good company with good people, and I had done everything that was asked of me! Nothing made sense.

I spiralled into questions: questions about my life and career that I had not answered; questions no one else had ever stopped to ask me. What makes me happy? What am I inspired by? What does contribution mean to me? What values is my life built on? What environments do I want to work in? Who do I want to learn from? What sacrifices am I prepared to make?

The only way forward was to tackle these compelling questions with honesty and courage. I resigned from my job and, stepped onto a new path with an unknown destination, ready to design my life on my terms.

*We all have the power of **choice**.*

• You have a choice about how you live your life, right now

• It is your responsibility to accept, make and own those choices

- When it goes right, celebrate, share and hone your skill

- When challenges arise, use them to grow

But, whatever happens... **don't hand over 10 years of your career to someone else's dream. No one is more equipped to be in the driver's seat of your life than you.**

AN INTRODUCTION TO VALUES

Values are defined as an important and enduring personal belief or ideal about what is good and desirable, and also what is not. Typically values are single words or short phrases - which we explore later in the chapter – and can be influenced by family, friends, spirituality, geography, economics and media (to name a few).

Throughout history, key events experienced by those in their formative years have driven what are known as generational value themes. Some examples include:

- Millenials (those born between the 1980's and the year 2000) grew up in a time where technology was freely available, during largely buoyant economic conditions and most often in dual income families. This has contributed to strong value structures around family, immediacy, choice and contribution.

- Generation-X (those born between the mid 1960's and the late 1970's) in contrast, have grown up through a period where the divorce rate increased from 20%-50% (increasing the number of single parent families) and the participation rate of women in the workforce increased from the mid 30% to nearly 60%. We have seen this translate to strong values around flexibility and work-life balance, particularly for those now raising young families of their own.

Values can change throughout time and the course of life. Young professionals in their 20's may see values such as freedom, travel, achievement and growth as what is most important during the early stages of their career lifecycle. As they progress into their 30's and

40's, and perhaps have a family of their own, values such as flexibility, security, stability and family may become more important.

Career values are significant because they impact on how you experience the workplace and sit behind your decisions. If you value *family* or *stability*, you may turn down a career with an organisation that mandates global mobility. Likewise, those who value *friendship* in context of their career will experience intense frustration, and most likely serious discontentment, in an organisation where competition and winning are highly praised.

A CASE STUDY IN LIVING YOUR VALUES

The impact of understanding your values is highlighted by the experience of a client who faced a difficult career decision. Two years into her role in a tough organisation, she was ready for a new opportunity and was invited to interview for a role with an interesting company. From the outset she was unsure if the role was right for her, but made a decision to see the process through to the end. Eventually, she was offered the job and with it, a $20,000 pay rise.

Money can be a blinding factor at the best of times and $20,000 for most people would and should be a serious consideration, but it is not the only factor to think about when it comes to career decisions. Values provide a much needed framework in what can be a highly emotional decision.

To help her unravel the situation, we completed the Career Values exercise which helped clarify what was most important to her at this stage of her career:

1. Freedom
2. Flexibility
3. Personal growth
4. Achievement
5. Social
6. Reputation

The simplicity of the process allowed her to compare, on paper, what she was feeling about both the current and potential role in a rational, conscious manner. Most importantly, it allowed her to understand what taking the new role would achieve beyond finances.

While our client knew the opportunity was not right from the beginning, money was hard to resist without sound reasoning. The values process provided insight into what the new role would and would not bring to her career and life. Armed with this knowledge, a confident **no** was easy and made without the 'what if?' onslaught.

ASK YOURSELF:
WHAT DO YOU VALUE?

Reconnecting with Core Confidence is not a linear process, but wherever you're at on the confidence journey, knowing what you value is essential. It is from this vantage point that you can begin to take aligned action.

HOW-TO:
YOUR CAREER VALUES

The career values exercise is an intuitive practice. This means we're going to connect with a deeper part of you beyond the conscious brain. As you are asked a series of questions, speak your natural and immediate answer rather than labouring in deep contemplation or overthinking. Get comfortable and let go of trying to *get it right*. You might surprise yourself.

As we begin, remember that a career value is an important and enduring personal belief or ideal about what is good or desirable, and what is not. It is a single word or short phrase that is meaningful **to you**.

Ask a friend, coach or mentor

Work with someone who can ask you the following questions (if you can't find anyone to do this with, work through this on your own, in a time and place when you can focus on the process).

Aligned action
is action that
honours your
values, skills and
future self

Be sure to answer naturally – focus on the words that capture the feeling or essence of your experience without getting hung up on their linguistic meaning.

Get ready

- Sit comfortably
- Close your eyes (to get out of the thinking brain)
- Have your friend ask you the series of questions below – reading directly from the instructions
- Ask your friend to write down your answers

Now, answer the questions

1. In one word, what is important to you in the area of CAREER

    1)

2. What else is important to you in context of CAREER (**Repeat 4 times**)

    2)
    3)
    4)
    5)

3. Now stop and remember a specific incident or time when you were totally motivated in the context of your CAREER? *(Wait to think of a time before moving on).* Keep your eyes closed, bring that specific time to mind and connect back in with the feelings, the sounds, and the pictures of being totally motivated in context of your career. As you go right back to that time, step into your body and see what you saw, hear what you heard and really feel the feelings of being totally motivated...and tell me...what was the name of the feelings or emotions that are present? *(Identify 1-2 responses)*

    6)
    7)

__Important:__ If you are facilitating the process for someone else allow them to use their own words. Do not give them ideas or suggestions.

Open your eyes and come back to the room

4. Review the list above (you may want to rewrite them in one list below) and make sure there are no two words that mean exactly the same thing to you. If this is the case, choose the one that resonates the most for you.

5. It is now time to rank the Career Values in order of priority of what is most important to you. One way to do this is with post it notes; move them around until you have your order with the first being what is most important.

GO DEEPER
WITH YOUR VALUES

One of the best ways to get a better understanding of your career values is to spend time reflecting on and writing about what specific values mean and why they are important to you. If you were surprised by the words that came up during the process, this extended exercise gives you the opportunity to uncover their origin and eventually speak with confidence about their meaning.

Writing (by hand) on a blank sheet of paper, select at least 3 of your values and spend some time responding to the question:

(INSERT VALUE) IS IMPORTANT TO ME BECAUSE.........

Continue to reflect on this question until you feel you have explored the value in enough detail, then move onto the next.

THE IMPACT OF GETTING HONEST WITH YOURSELF

There is a direct and powerful link between clarity and confidence:

- When things get tough or you feel threatened – knowing your values helps you maintain the motivation to continue on (and even risk rejection or failure) because your values are worth it

- When opportunities are present – knowing your values helps you identify those worth pursuing and take action, even if it feels like a stretch or a little scary

- When you need to say not yet – knowing your values helps you say **no** to what is not important. With so many competing priorities, you can have it all – but you can't have it all at the same time. We must learn to say no to some things or as we prefer to say "not yet" or "not today"

The process toward clarity does not happen overnight, nor is it the only component of Core Confidence. Unpacking what lights you up in the context of career (and using this insight to take aligned action) is a necessary and meaningful starting point.

Be your own coach

Once you have language to express your values, consider the following:

- How are your Career Values impacting your workplace experience? Assess your values against your current workplace experience, i.e. on a scale of 1 to 10 where 10 is as much of the value as you could ever dream of and 1 is no amount of the value

- Reflect on a time in your career when you were loving what you were doing. How did this opportunity align with your Career Values? Why?

- How are your Career Values impacting your career decisions? Is your current role moving you more towards your career values or away from them?

- How aligned are your Career Values with the values of the organisation you work for?

- Are there any conflicts internally within your values, eg. by pursing your value of *progression* you move away from your value of *flexibility*. If so what strategies can you implement to help navigate these conflicts?

- How do your Career Values fit into other areas / aspects of life that are important to you?

NOTES

NOTES

GET CLEAR

Chapter 2

SET GOALS &
TAKE ACTION

By recording your *dreams and goals* on paper, you set in motion the process of becoming the person you most *want* to be. Put your *future* in good hands... your own

- Mark Victor Hansen

In a world where there is no end to the tasks you could busy yourself with, identifying and prioritising the types of experiences you wish to have is a necessity. With your values clarified, it is time to create a plan that focuses your finite energy and resources.

TO GOAL OR NOT TO GOAL

On some level, we know that most people have set goals before, mostly in relation to their work and performance plans. It is for this reason that goal setting has suffered a bad rap in terms of effectiveness.

Yet, top level athletes, successful businesspeople and high achievers in all fields set goals. They do this because a well defined goal provides both long term vision and short term motivation– bringing your current and future selves together in a way like no other.

A frequently referenced study from Harvard conducted in 1979 attributes the process of writing goals down as the reason why 3% of Harvard MBAs make ten times as much as the other 97% combined. Attempts to source the study revealed it to be a myth, however subsequent research has validated that when goals are written down they are far more likely to manifest in reality[17].

MOVING YOUR GOALS FROM HEAD TO PAPER

When goals remain lost in thought, they lose their power. Instead of being a source of continued inspiration and focus, goals can compete with each other in the mind and become a source of stress. For this reason, it's important to articulate in a simple and measurable way, on paper, what you're trying to achieve and how you'll celebrate when you get there.

Before we move from head to paper, there's another trick to this process that we need to talk about: make decisions about your goals in a timely manner and stick to them! We watch perfectionism and fear act as barriers to creating a plan. Your goals are designed to challenge you to extend yourself, learn and grow. You'll need to trust your abilities, information, intelligences (we'll explore these soon) and values to set them. Write your goals down, paste them all over your house and.. go for it!

> *"Successful people make decisions quickly (as soon as all the facts are available) and change them very slowly (if ever). Unsuccessful people make decisions very slowly, and change them often and quickly."*

> *- Napolean Hill*

Let us share some of the goal setting techniques that have worked for our clients. Our desire is not to simply tell you what you already know, but to encourage you to put what you know **to use** and create the life you want.

HOW-TO:
YOUR WHEEL OF LIFE

The first step in effective goal setting is to observe which areas of life need specific attention. The wheel of life enables you to visualise the areas that may be out of balance or need a little attention, to set goals and priorities accordingly.

Start here

Create space (physically, emotionally and mentally) and make the time to connect in with what is most important to you. Think about the sort of life you want to live and legacy you want to create (refer to the values process in Chapter 1). This *dreamlike* thinking is different to how many of us spend our day, so put yourself in a different state and environment to follow this process. We suggest going to your favourite place by the ocean or in the sun with some coloured pens and blank paper to get the creative energy flowing.

Powerful decisions require trust in your ability, intelligences and values

Get creative

1. Draw a big circle to fill a page, and draw lines to separate it into seven wedge shapes. Label each wedge with a topic area that is important to your life. You can choose topic areas from one of the lists below, or create your own. Select areas of life that are most important to you right now. Trust your instincts here.

Professional

- Career
- Leadership
- Influence
- Negotiation
- Networking
- Communication
- Confidence
- Personal Brand

Personal

- Personal Growth
- Relationships
- Health & Well-being
- Finances
- Fun & Recreation
- Professional
- Development
- Significant Other
- Self belief
- Friends
- Family

2. As in the pictured wheel circle below, imagine that the inner axis of the wheel spokes represents a score of zero. The outer edge of the circle represents the top score of five. Now rate each wedge according to how fulfilled you feel in that area. A score of zero indicates that you have no focus, progress or success in that area of your life. A score of five indicates that you are content, focused, and consistently achieving all your goals in that area. Score by drawing a dotted line across the wedge to represent where you are now, and a solid line to represent where you would like to be.

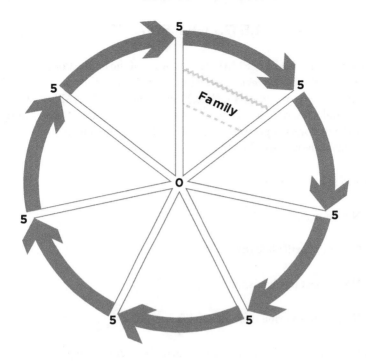

This process will help you identify areas of life that could do with some extra attention. When I (Kate) first completed this process, my wheel was anything but an evenly proportioned circle. In areas like career and finances I was nailing it. On most of my other areas (intimate relationships, health, fun and personal growth) I was a pretty much out of the game scoring a one or two at best.

The wheel of life activity holistically honours how each element contributes to the successful functioning of the whole. To enjoy the ride, we need, over time, to have fully functioning and performing parts. Well rounded and balanced individuals not only perform better professionally but are more fulfilled in their personal life as well.

Think about the impact of my wheel of life; with only two out of seven fully functioning wedges – and the remaining sections flat and lifeless. It was a rough time. Flat spots on your wheel of life can help identity which areas to prioritise when you begin to set your own goals.

LET'S GET SMART

You may have heard of SMART goals, again in the context of your annual performance review. We want you to look at this method with fresh eyes. For many years I, (Kate) was dismissive of SMART without truly understanding the technique. In my coaching capacity, I began to see the reasons people were failing to achieve the targets they had set for themselves, even when they had great enthusiasm:

• Too many goals

• Not enough clarity

• Could not articulate the benefits

• No support mechanisms

• No system to bring their idea to life

The word SMART is an acronym with each letter standing for a characteristic of a well set goal, and it is a methodology that enables you to create a meaningful future.

BREAKING SMART INTO PIECES

S is for **Specific**. State exactly what you want to achieve, focusing on the W's: Who, What, When, and Where. It is important that you are very clear about what you want to achieve. For example, you may want to work without distraction—no email, phone, social media or meetings—for 60 minutes a day. Try specifically identifying the time of day that you will implement this distraction free period. By narrowing your goal with laser-like precision, you will easily be able to assess whether or not you can achieve it. If a goal isn't specific enough, you may find yourself wasting time wondering whether you are making progress.

M is for **Measurable**. There is an old adage—what gets measured, gets done. If you can measure your progress with a starting point and an end goal, then you can track progress, which can help when the effort you are putting in does not feel like it is making much of a difference. Of course it becomes very clear when you have achieved your end point or goal.

A is for **Achievable**. An achievable goal is one where you have a reasonable chance of reaching the goal successfully. When it comes to setting a goal, you have to consider who you are (what you are capable of), the nature of the habit you want to change or goal you want to achieve and the environment in which you operate. We often caution people about setting radical targets or *stretch* goals when undertaking this process. Stretch goals have largely been discounted as a strategy for success, as most people not only failed to achieve these goals, but became disheartened and lost faith and confidence in their ability to achieve their goals. Far more success is achieved with smaller wins over a shorter period of time, like staircasing your way to the top of a mountain as compared to climbing the steep cliff.

R is for **Relevant**. The importance of this one is huge and probably the most potent! Unless the goal is relevant to your journey, you may find yourself asking: "why bother at all?". Without a compelling why, interest in your goal is likely to wane over the long run, and motivation and effort decrease. Ultimately you might give up. Make sure your driving reason is strong enough to support the focus and energy it will take to achieve your goal.

T is for **Time bound**. Setting a completion date or deadline will help prioritise your energy and attention (both limited resources). Be realistic with this date and perhaps even set small goals or milestone dates so that you can achieve success on a more frequent basis.

HOW-TO:
BRINGING IT ALL TOGETHER

Review your wheel of life and identify three areas that you would most like to change or improve. Create three goals – one for each of your life areas – using the SMART methodology to ensure they are achievable. Remember to write your goals down!

To help, here is one we prepared earlier....

Over the coming 6 months, I will speak up more (at least 3-5 times) in monthly marketing project meetings for example ask questions, volunteer to present, contribute to discussion points, so that the senior leaders (Stakeholder A, Stakeholder B, Stakeholder C) can see my knowledge and expertise in the areas of digital marketing and begin to ask my advice and include me on more discussions outside this meeting. Ultimately this will improve my influence and brand within the organisation and provide access to higher order projects that will build experience on my resume.

Once you are clear about your goals develop a plan of action:

- Prioritise and breakdown your goal into quarterly, monthly and weekly actions and diarise these – if it's not scheduled it doesn't happen

- Keep your goals close – proximity is power when it comes to knowing and focusing on your goals. Have your goals printed out and stuck in areas around your home; make them a screen saver on your phone or computer or even write them on your mirror (you can get special pens for this)

- Share your goals with a friend or trusted colleague. Being held accountable by a person other than yourself is an incredibly powerful force when it comes to driving action. It is easy to make excuses to ourselves. It is much harder to say it out loud to someone who we respect and whose opinion we value

- Regularly sit down and review how you are progressing with your goals. Doing this weekly can ensure that roadblocks are addressed and momentum maintained. If you are not making progress ask yourself some honest questions. What's not working? What are the obstacles in your way? Time (when), Motivation (why), Knowledge (how), Beliefs, Money..... Identify these and create a strategy to overcome them when they get in the way.

If it's *important* you
will find a *way*,
if it's not you will
find an *excuse*!

CONFIDENCE APPEARS ON A WINDING ROAD

Whenever laziness arises or momentum wanes, simply ask the question: Is this important? If the answer is **yes** then action needs to be taken.

The road to confidence is bumpy and there is a perception gap between what we think it takes to be successful and what it actually takes.

SUCCESS

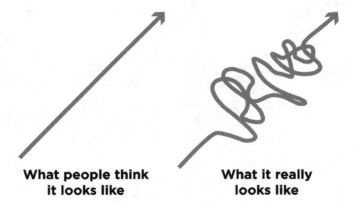

What people think it looks like

What it really looks like

Be your own coach

- We know there will be days where you will want to say "who cares about these goals anyway?" Allow those days to happen, go to bed and wake up promising yourself to bring a fresh attitude the next day

- Connect in with your driving reasons; why your goals matter, why they are important to you; and revisit your plan. In our experience this is the best way to get back on the horse and keep moving forward

- When you achieve a milestone on your journey, celebrate what you have achieved and, importantly, who you are becoming

NOTES

NOTES

SET GOALS & TAKE ACTION

Chapter 3

KNOW YOUR STUFF

When it comes
to *confidence*,
knowledge is *power*,
but not quite how
you *think*

Many clients hold a deep belief that to have *more* confidence, they need to *know* more. Yet, no amount of information cramming the night before an important meeting is enough to safeguard these high achievers from their lack of self belief. And herein lies the problem.

Driven by the fear of not knowing, capable people are aspiring to be the person who never has to ask a silly question or, better still, the person who has the answers to every possible question.

To loosen our grip on knowing it all, we're going to introduce you to the concepts of *grounded expertise* and *growth mindset*. We will give you the tools and inspiration that enable you to embrace the technology and dynamics of 21st Century workplaces.

THE TRAGEDY OF SILENCE

Too often we see and hear about female professionals curtailing their contribution in meetings because they are not the expert, even when they:

• are respected professionals in their organisation

• offer valuable insights

• have interesting questions to expand the discussion

• are across the latest research in their discipline

• possess a great desire to learn more

With such an impressive array of attributes, everyone loses when these women remain quiet.

In her 2016 TED Talk *Teach girls bravery, not perfection*[18], Reshma Saujani tells the story of young men and women studying Computer Sciences at the University of Columbia asking for help with their assignment: male students say "Professor, something is wrong with my code", while female students say "Professor, something is wrong with me". Suajani calls it a female *bravery deficit* born of social construction that limits the participation of highly competent, knowledgeable women.

In the context of confidence, it's time to look at the role of expertise with a new lens and challenge our silence.

EXPERTISE IS AN **AND** CONVERSATION

Through our research and personal experience we have learned that knowledge gathering alone is an external and fraught approach to developing confidence. While important for career advancement, wanting to know everything (before participating) is a practice that lulls professionals into a false sense of security or insecurity, with consequences such as:

Silence or an inability to perform
If you hold the belief that you don't know enough, you may struggle to enter the conversation or take part in meetings or activities

Arrogance
If you hold the belief that knowledge alone protects you from change or guarantees success

Anxiety
If you hold the belief that *not enough knowledge* translates into *I'm not enough*

The truth is, in today's world, experts (in the traditional sense of the word) are extremely rare. Their mastery of a subject is the result of questioning, practice, failure, sacrifice and discipline; qualities that are not beyond any of us, should we choose to invest in them.

Expertise is a paradox: knowledge is important and yet on its own is not enough to sustain confidence. It is vital to learn everything you can with the time you have, be aware of potential questions or gaps and collaborate with others to expand your ideas, rather than trying to have all the solutions yourself.

ADAPTABILITY IS A 21ST CENTURY SUPER POWER

In an era when information is ubiquitous and new discoveries are being published daily, subject matter expertise has become *a ticket to play* rather than a pure advantage and while you need to know your stuff, what you need to know could turn on a dime.

The World Economic Forum predicts that five million jobs will be lost by 2020 – a staggering statistic that highlights the need for the ability to adapt, and fast. What is being termed *"The Fourth Industrial Revolution"* has already begun with disruption to entire industries reshaping the world we work and live in. As a result, over 35% of core skills are estimated to change by 2020[19].

So, in this new world, how can you use your strengths, education, personal and technical skills, authenticity and resilience to propel you forward?

START BY GETTING GROUNDED

The word *expert* is derived from the Latin word *expereri* which means *to find out or prove* and acts as the base of the word *experience*. Grounded is associated with the Old English word *grund*, translating into *the foundation*.

Grounded expertise is defined then as subject matter knowledge and skill supported by self awareness and emotional intelligence. It is a critical feature of confidence and created through two primary mechanisms:

1. Your approach to your discipline

- Passionate enquiry and intrigue about your subject
- Competence in your field
- Experimentation
- Ability to challenge the status quo
- Effective collaboration
- Failing fast and learning

Grounded *expertise* is all about knowing your subject and yourself simultaneously

2. Your approach to your development

- Integrating the components of core confidence
- Developing your interpersonal skills
- Tackling unique and interesting challenges

Grounded expertise is the middle road, ensuring you don't get too far ahead of yourself with what you know or disabled by what you don't.

WITH A HEALTHY FOUNDATION, CREATE YOUR NICHE (WHAT DO YOU WANT TO BE KNOWN FOR?)

Now the fun begins. Once you let go of needing to know it all, you can fire up your passion for learning, explore what you love and discover what sets you apart. In the new world of work, it's going to be critical to know what you have to offer, so let's get clear about where you shine bright.

HOW-TO:
DISCOVERING YOUR NICHE

Think about possible answers to the questions below and see if you can start to identify your own niche.

1. Which area of your work is so fascinating to you that you would be happy researching and working on it for years into the future?

2. What area of your field gives you a sense that you have something new and worthwhile to contribute?

3. Which areas do you find yourself naturally defending or standing up for? What are you already spending your energy on?

Defining your niche is an essential step in creating your personal brand.

Personal brand is the means by which other people remember you

HAVE A VOICE

In a how-to guide, we couldn't miss the opportunity to talk about communication and confidence. It is no use living your niche, without also being able to share your knowledge in a way that is relevant to your peers, industry and community.

Your behaviour, the commitments you make, email language, meeting interactions, LinkedIn posts – in fact, all facets of who you are and how you show up communicate your personal brand to anyone who is paying attention. We coach our clients to become conscious about what they want to be remembered for and get deliberate about the message they are sending. In this arena, there are two components:

Audience (who you are talking to)

Knowing which groups of people you seek to influence and reaching them is part of building your profile and brand.

Think of the people you want to be able to influence:

1. What matters to them?

2. Where are they (in person and online)?

3. How will you add to, shift or extend their current perspective?

Communication (how you are talking to your audience)

When you are clear about your niche and know who you want to reach, it is time to start regularly communicating with your audience in interesting and authentic ways.

1. Look for situations to talk and listen to others

2. When opportunities arise, speak up and say yes to invitations to share your knowledge and perspective. This may be both inside your organisation and/or within industry groups or communities

3. Share relevant articles and research or develop something of your own to publish (LinkedIn can be a great platform for this)

DIFFERENT TYPES OF KNOWING
ALICIA'S STORY

Alicia was always a high achiever; she received top marks in high school and at university. She started her career with a multi national property developer and found the work stimulating and exciting. After five years working in various roles throughout the business, she landed her dream opportunity in corporate social responsibility. Now she could make a difference; she'd be able to influence the corporate world with the knowledge and skill she had gained during her education and over the past five years.

Three months into her new role, Alicia was asked to present the ideas her team had been working on for the next financial year, to the CEO and group executive (a team of approximately 15 people). Alicia was excited to share all the knowledge she had researched, the reasons they had selected these particular activities and how it would impact the brand's positive standing in the wider community.

Armed with statistics, reports, handouts and a killer slide-deck, Alicia felt she was prepared for anything. Three slides into her presentation some of the executive started to raise questions: "What's the Return on Investment (ROI) on this activity?", "Have you fully calculated the risk to the business if this initiative fails?" and "We're not social workers – this stuff doesn't relate to our business!" Unprepared for the robust questioning and debate she encountered, Alicia at first tried to steer back to the subject of her presentation and when that didn't work, she defended the proposals and ideas.

Rather than welcoming their questions and seeing it as an opportunity to broaden the conversation and get new ideas on the table, Alicia felt their questions were an attack on her professionalism. In trying to defend the team's position she felt as though she *should* have all the answers and that not having them immediately undermined her confidence.

A GROWTH MINDSET MATTERS MORE THAN EVER

In the current era, where information is freely available at the tap of a finger, being an expert is only possible if you are prepared to commit to being a lifelong learner. Your expertise remains valuable and relevant as you continue to expand your knowledge and connect it to other important trends and ideas.

An essential aspect to lifelong learning is having a *growth mindset* rather than a *fixed mindset*. Carol Dweck, of Stanford University[20], is recognised as the originator of this concept. She found that what really differentiates people beyond talent and knowledge is their mindset.

Those with a *fixed mindset* feel they have to constantly prove their expertise and talent – they want to always have the answer. All decisions are guided by the thought of being evaluated for what they already have and already know. Often, people secretly know that they cannot always be perfect or know the answer, so they become fearful of being found out.

A *growth mindset*, however, is concerned with what is possible – where to from here? This perspective holds that whatever you have is a starting point and from here you will expand and build your capacity and talents over your lifetime. These people are free from the constraint of having to *know it all* or being seen as perfect; they know that being challenged and not always having the right answer stretches them to grow.

This leads to one of the greatest challenges for modern day experts – the ability and willingness to accept that, despite all the knowledge, learning and hard work, often over many, many years, someone else is likely to surpass that expert understanding. To be able to navigate this experience will require you to let go of the need to be right.

Letting go of the need to be right

It is human to want to prove that you are right and to strongly defend that position. Whilst it may feel confronting at times (possibly every time), experimenting with this part of you, can be a powerful personal and professional development opportunity.

Try the following:

- Be curious about diverse and dissenting perspectives – get all the views out in the open and evaluate the strengths of each

- Be prepared to let go of your previously held opinion when challenged

- Ask yourself and others, "what other perspectives could be valid?"

There's a sweet spot between taking a stand and becoming defensive, and it often occurs in the space of letting go of the need to be right. To develop professionally and personally, you need to be willing to try new things, speak up, take risks and get it wrong over and over again.

Be your own coach

- Get curious about your grounded expertise: What's your passion? Where is your niche?

- Know your audience and what matters to them

- Develop a *growth mindset* by seeing situations and challenges as learning experiences

- Explore informal learning opportunities (reading, podcasts, videos, online courses)

- Let go of the need to be right – seek to collaborate more and ask questions to explore different perspectives in an open way

- Build relationships and collaborate where possible with experts in your industry. Learning from others can be one of the best ways to keep up to date and contribute to new thinking in your field

- Know your stuff AND be ok with not knowing everything

NOTES

NOTES

Chapter 4

WORK HARD
(STRATEGICALLY)

There is an unconscious link between the *value* of something and the *effort* it took to achieve it

We have been taught to believe that if something comes easily, then it is not worth having. Not surprisingly then, we find pride in the struggle, long hours and hard work endured to achieve our goals.

The problem is hard work has become indistinguishable from *overworking* leading to talented, high performing women burning out. With the potential for significant health, relationship and career impacts, we need to get strategic about how we work.

THE CULTURE OF HARD WORK

Technology has increased the speed with which we receive information and how quickly others expect replies. At the same time, the volume of information available has made it virtually impossible to review all documents and make decisions in a time efficient manner.

Meetings and other *important* work related activities take up a larger portion of the working week, while corporate restructures have tripled the tasks, skills and capabilities required to do our day-to-day job. With so many competing priorities, there isn't enough time to get everything done and so we work longer.

Many organisational cultures have been built on the back of *long hours* defining high performance. Yet, in a study of consultants by Erin Reid, a professor at Boston University's Questrom School of Business, managers could not tell the difference between employees who actually worked 80 hours a week and those who just pretended to. And, while managers penalised employees who were transparent about working less, Reid was not able to find any evidence that those employees actually accomplished less, or any sign that the overworking employees accomplished more[21].

So, why aren't long hours and hard work, creating a clear difference between us and those who are less invested?

In our coaching work we ask a powerful question: For what *purpose* and at what *cost*?

Hard work is not always valuable work

Working hard doesn't always make your work more valuable. We each have aspects of our role that add more value or are more important than perhaps routine or repetitive activities. Employees are required to make choices about how they spend their time and energy, which means there is a continual trade off between what they are not doing because they are choosing to do something else. Pouring more hours into a task doesn't necessarily make those hours or outcomes more valuable.

Hard work is not always creative work

Hard work doesn't necessarily yield creativity. Some of our best ideas come in isolated moments of nothing. Think about the last time you had a great idea? In the shower, on the treadmill or strolling in the park on the way home? Great ideas don't always flow when 10 people are sitting around a boardroom table with flipchart paper, markers and an instruction to "be creative". Ideas come in spontaneous moments, often when we are accessing the incredible power of our whole brain. In a world where creativity, innovation and collaboration are the currencies of success, learning how to harness this power – beyond locking ourselves in a room for 12 hours – is critical.

Hard work is not always healthy

I (Kate) am the first to hold up my hand and say that even to this day I am still unconsciously tied to the belief that working hard equals success. Give me a deadline and you can guarantee I will meet it! I'll work through the night if I have to, to guarantee the outcome will be delivered. Feeling sick? If it's got to get done, it will get done, even if I am in bed with my lap top and a nasty bout of tonsillitis: it has been done.

It was only when my addiction to hard work (and the rewards of getting things done) started costing me my health, sending me on a fast track to burn out and adrenal fatigue, that I began to rethink my approach.

Hard work is exhausting and it doesn't take long for it to catch up with you. Numerous studies have found that overwork and the resulting stress can lead to all sorts of mental, physical and social health problems, including disrupted sleep, depression, heavy drinking, diabetes, fractured relationships with our partners, children and friends, impaired memory and heart disease.

And, it's not good for the company's health either. Hard work and fatigue show up on the bottom line as absenteeism, turnover and presentism (when someone is on the job but for various reasons not fully functioning)[22].

Hard work won't guarantee progression

We have seen many women create impressive careers from working hard, making significant compromises in other aspects of life to achieve success. But, we all know someone (perhaps even you have experienced this) who works hard, is brilliant at what they do and yet is passed over for promotion time and time again. When we're busy working hard, it's easy to forget the skills, relationships and attributes we need to develop for our next role.

Hard work does not mean perfect

Perfectionism is a no win game; it hampers achievement and is correlated with depression, anxiety, addiction, and life paralysis or missed opportunities. Despite this, many women measure their performance (and appearance) against this unrealistic ideal – attempting to be a perfect career woman, friend, daughter, mother and so on.

Dr. Brené Brown, research professor at the University of Houston Graduate College of Social Work, as well as a #1 New York Times bestselling author, talks at length about both perfectionism and vulnerability. She says perfectionism is the belief that if we do things perfectly, we can minimise the pain of blame, judgement or shame and ultimately earn the approval of others[23]. Perfectionism is very different to self improvement; the underlying drive for perfectionists is that their identity is completely determined by how well they accomplish every task.

Learning how to move an idea or project forward without the trappings of *perfection* is a *critical* skill

HOW TO:
WORK STRATEGICALLY

We want to share work habits with you that promote a healthy
exchange between you and your workplace. These are the strategies we
use to move our clients from a passive experience of *overworked* and
overwhelmed to an empowered approach of focus, productivity and
energy.

1. *Know your priorities*

Ask yourself: what is important? Check in with your values and
goals, and work with senior stakeholders to understand the most
pressing issues to be across. Then, allocate your resources, such as
time, appropriately. Be intentional about *what* you'll focus on, and
practise letting the small stuff go. Not everything will get done when it
is supposed to get done. If you are focused on the right things, it won't
matter.

2. *Plan*

This is the *when*. Plan how you will spend your time rather than
giving it away. Be conscious of and eliminate distractions. The most
dangerous distractions are those that you do not recognise – meetings,
emails and other incidental work-related activity. Your 40 (or 50) hour
work week can easily be monopolised by the demands of others if you
let it. Once you know what is most important, diarise it.

We love Stephen Covey's teaching in this area (His books include
First Things First and *Seven Habits of Highly Effective People*).
Covey's famous example references a bucket (which symbolises our
life), a few big rocks (which symbolise our important priorities) and
a bunch of small pebbles (which symbolise the urgent, busy tasks that
aren't important). In front of an audience, he pours the pebbles into
the bucket, and instructs an audience member to fit the big rocks
in afterward which, of course, is impossible to do. Covey then takes
everything out and starts again. He puts the big rocks into the bucket
first, pouring the pebbles in afterward. The pebbles fill the cracks left

between the big rocks, allowing the participant to fit everything into the bucket[24].

The metaphor is clear; focus on the priorities and everything else will fall into place, focus on tasks and you'll miss out on what's important.

3. *One thing at a time*

Don't do it all at once or at least create some space in the day where you can focus on a single project or task. As much as you think you are getting more done, multitasking is the quickest way to drain mental energy with little return. Our brains can only do one conscious thing at a time; switching between tasks not only wastes energy but leads to decreased performance and an increase in mistakes.

Not convinced? Try this small test:

1. Draw two horizontal lines on a piece of paper

2. Now, have someone time you as you carry out the two tasks that follow:

   a. On the first line write: I am a great multitasker

   b. On the second line write: the numbers 1-20 sequentially, like those below:

   1 2 3 4 5 6 7 8 9 10 11 12 13 14 15 16 17 18 19 20

   How much time did it take to do the two tasks? Usually it's about 20 seconds.

3. Now, let's multitask. Draw two more horizontal lines. This time, (again have someone time you) write a letter on one line, and then a number on the line below, then the next letter in the sentence on the upper line, and then the next number in the sequence, changing from line to line. In other words, you write the letter "I" and then the number "1" and then the letter "a" and then the number "2" and so on, until you complete both lines.

We bet when multitasking your time is double or more what it was on the first round. You also may have made some errors and you were probably frustrated since you had to re-think what the next letter would be and then the next number.

While doing more than one thing, at one time, may feel like efficiency, very rarely is this the case. Start to make conscious and intentional choices about what you will choose to give your attention to and give yourself a time limit to focus on just one task. See if you can't complete it better, faster and with less energy.

4. *Know your strengths*

"People who use their strengths every day are more than three times more likely to report having an excellent quality of life and six times more likely to be engaged at work." [25]

To boost your productivity, invest in pursuits that complement your natural strengths. If you're not good at something, don't enjoy it and don't want to learn more about it – why are you doing it? Recruit the skills of others for those tasks and channel your talents into high impact areas. That said, and as you already know, there will always be mundane requirements that you must complete, but this should only ever be 20-30% of your role, to ensure that your time, skills and capabilities are being put to good use.

5. *Work with your biology*

Know your body and use your peak times of concentration. A few years ago, a colleague and I (Kate) researched productivity and workplace distraction. At the time, our hypothesis was that the current workplace makes it very difficult to be productive and we were wanting to explore the impact of this on organisations and employees. The results showed that 47% of people are completely unproductive five or more hours a week[26] and this is just the tip of the iceberg when it comes to how the modern day worker manages their time and energy. Become curious about when you feel most productive or can focus best. Use this genius time for difficult, challenging or creative work and save the time when you have limited mental or emotional capacity for those aspects of your job that are less demanding.

6. *Habits are your friend*

Build your autopilot function. The human brain is a wonderful and awe-inspiring thing and we still don't fully understand how the brain and human body operates. What we do know is that the brain loves efficiency and where possible will develop habits that help us function effectively. Driving, brushing our teeth, logging onto our computers, using operating systems in our lines of work are all activities that when repeated often enough become automatic and use minimal attention and memory stores. This is powerful. You can create routine habits and rituals that allow you to complete tasks without conscious thought and conserve your precious energy and cognitive function.

7. *Ask for help*

In Chapter 9 we explore how to Ask for Help and the barriers that can sometimes get in the way. Make no mistake: the support of others (and providing support to others) is one of the most powerful ways to work strategically. Serial entrepreneur Richard Branson, says that "success in business is all about making connections".

8. *Take care of yourself*

There's nothing more important than how you take care of yourself. Stephen Covey tells a story about a woodcutter whose saw gets blunter as he cuts down trees. If the woodcutter were to stop sawing, sharpen his saw, and go back to cutting the tree with a sharp blade, he would actually save time and effort in the long run. Covey notes "Sharpen the Saw means preserving and enhancing the greatest asset you have, you. It means having a balanced program for self-renewal in the four areas of your life: physical, social/emotional, mental, and spiritual"[27]. Sharpening the Saw is a great habit to adopt in all areas of your life, but is especially important to avoid burnout.

9. *Leverage the night shift*

Most of us dramatically underestimate the work that our brain does overnight. Unlike a computer that is shut down, your brain goes to work when you go to sleep. If you deprive your brain of this opportunity, your performance will be impacted. Let's look at three incredible things your brain does while you're sleeping:

1) **Processes information** - The brain can process information and prepare for action during sleep, effectively making decisions while unconscious. In fact, for complex decisions research shows us that *sleeping on it* will deliver better results than investing more awake time deliberating.

2) **Makes and consolidates memories** - Lack of rest can have a significant impact on the hippocampus, an area of the brain involved in memory creation and consolidation. For this reason, sleep plays a vital role in learning, it helps us to cement the new information we're taking in for better recall.

3) **Creates connections** - The mind in an unconscious resting state can make surprising new connections that it perhaps wouldn't have made in a waking state. A study by University of California, Berkeley, reported by the BBC[28], found that sleep can foster *remote associates*, or unusual connections, in the brain which could lead to a major "a-ha" moment upon waking.

Sleep is essential for healthy functioning of body, mind and soul, and is powerful in enabling connections and solutions that do not occur in a waking state.

WORK HARD STRATEGICALLY

Let's face it, to get somewhere meaningful in life, you need to pour your heart, mind and energy into the endeavour. Working hard is a necessity for both our sense of self and our success. *How* you work and rest, however, is a choice and determines how far you can go.

Be your own coach

- Think about your current role and organisational priorities – what are the top three to five projects or outcomes that you need to get done in the next week, month or quarter (use what is most relevant)? It can be useful to check these with your boss to make sure you are on the same page

- Reflect on the priorities above - how much time of your available work week did you spend working explicitly on these tasks? What is one thing you could do to prioritise the amount of time and energy you give to these tasks next week?

- Do your workplace habits make you more or less productive? What one thing could you start or stop doing that would enhance your productivity on a daily basis?

- What are your strengths? Take the Clifton Strengths test *(https://www.gallupstrengthscenter.com/)* if you need language about your natural talents and begin to explore how you can use them (and what to let go of that does not interest or benefit you and your organisation)

- What time of day do you feel most productive or effective when it comes to doing work that requires deep thinking? How could you structure your day to leverage this?

- Who is on your team? Get clear about what you are good at and identify three to five people who you can develop strong and supportive relationships in the workplace to help shortcut each other to success

- Develop a self-care routine and plan. Identify one small activity that can support your body and brain to maintain its genius physically, emotionally and mentally

- Reflect on your relationship with sleep and identify how it can support you to be even more brilliant than you are today. This may include improving the quality or cycle of sleep patterns or how you leverage your unconscious processing capacity while you sleep

NOTES

WORK HARD (STRATEGICALLY)

NOTES

Chapter 5

BUILD
RELATIONSHIPS

The adage *it's not what you know, it's who you know* is as relevant today as ever

As the working world continues to change, your ability to collaborate and cooperate to achieve your own and the organisation's goals will be even more important.

Olivia is an accomplished business analyst; she studied hard at university, and in her first two roles in the corporate sector honed her skills and talents. Olivia is often called on to give her opinion because she has a strong grasp of technology and business fundamentals. Although she is well regarded, Olivia often feels isolated and unable to really connect with those she would like to influence beyond her immediate team.

Sabine is a skillful operator, a strong leader and a collaborative contributor to the executive team. She is also highly respected and her input is sought after for projects across the organisation. Sabine is well connected and engages with her networks both internally and broadly across the industry and business community.

Both these women are intelligent, highly adept at their work and well regarded, yet Sabine is earning significantly more and is earmarked as a high potential future leader in the business. At the same time, Olivia is seen as a specialist who, while contributing well, does not have the interpersonal skills for senior leadership. What accounts for this difference?

We know that a key factor in suitability for leadership positions is the capacity to build and sustain strong relationships. While both Sabine and Olivia are talented, Sabine has invested considerable time in building a strong network of relationships both within and beyond her organisation. Olivia's circle of influence is limited, while Sabine has far higher visibility and is perceived as having greater potential. This perception aids her personal growth and confidence, while Olivia is left questioning why she can't make headway.

As your career evolves, the ability to create enduring relationships will be an essential component to progression. If meeting new people sounds daunting, let us show you the value of overcoming that fear and developing your personal network.

NATURAL NETWORKING

Building relationships is often confused with its distant cousin *networking*; a term that has unfairly gained a lot of bad press over the years. Traditional approaches to networking often require a staunch dedication to working the room, making the most of each introduction or moving along quickly to maximise the number of contacts reached at each event. The focus on this type of connection is about asking "What can you do for me?"

Most people find this old school idea of networking off-putting and unlikely to build lasting and productive relationships. So, breathe a sigh of relief! You no longer have to worry about giving business cards to as many people as you can at a function, while simultaneously rushing to share your *elevator pitch* as many times as possible.

Today, professional networking is about being your natural self in order to create a genuine connection with another person. Without the pressure of fast and superficial encounters, there is space to get to know someone on a deeper level and acknowledge the skills, industry network and insights you both bring to the table.

The benefits of natural networking are mutual:

1. Learning from each other's experience and knowledge

2. Recommending skills, knowledge and expertise to your shared networks and associates

3. Bolstering self worth when faced with a crisis by reminding each other of your resilience and accomplishments

4. Providing insightful feedback in areas for improvement or development

5. Harnessing the power of *we* – in relationships with others we are able to create something greater than each person could do on their own

HOW-TO:
CREATE STRONG RELATIONSHIPS

1. *Start with you*

We know that confidence itself is very much an inner game. This is also true of relationships. Without a relationship with yourself, and the self awareness that arises as a result, it is difficult to build, sustain and contribute to relationships with others.

We discuss this idea further in Chapter 8, Be Authentic, but the salient point is that the more you know who you are, including your values and strengths, the more confidence you will have in the company of others.

2. *Develop your communication style*

Being a great communicator is crucial when building relationships. There is no way we can do this subject justice in such a small segment, so, here we're highlighting the basics.

Effective communication is defined as *when your message has been received as intended.* Given people communicate in different ways, you may need to adjust your communication style to truly connect with your audience in each context. As an interaction unfolds, tune in to how the other person is responding and the meaning they are making from the exchange.

Great communication requires a balance between talking and listening; being open and sharing what is on your mind and listening intently to understand what the other person is saying. This fosters a two-way exchange. Active listening is an art, and takes a real desire to hear what is being said beyond words. By listening to what is said, and what is unsaid, you can more deeply understand what matters to the person you are talking to.

To improve your communication, ask yourself these questions about a recent exchange:

- Were you both focused and present, without distractions during the conversation?

- Did you understand what the other person wanted or needed in the situation?

- Were you clear about what you were trying to communicate?

- Did you plan your key messages to overcome nerves?

- If not, what questions could you have asked to get clarity about that?

- Was there anything being implied subtly in the conversation that needs to be explicitly discussed?

- Was the other person clear about what you wanted or needed?

- What did their body language tell you?

- How did you check that they fully understand what matters to you?

- Was there anything unsaid that was inhibiting communication between you?

While much of the above sounds more like common sense, busy minds, workplace distractions and a lack of planning means that we walk into most conversations without being clear about what we want. We forget to pay attention to the unspoken message, instead thinking about what is coming up later on in the day. Planning what you want to communicate, especially if the message is complex or likely to inspire conflict, is crucial.

3. *Be strategic*

Some relationships happen without conscious effort – we easily get to know people we studied with or have worked with and they naturally become friends, mentors, collaborators and sounding boards. These relationships tend to build organically over time, you choose to stay in touch because you have a shared history and a strong connection.

Other relationships will require a more strategic approach. Depending on your purpose and goals, there are likely to be people who you currently don't know or don't know well, who could be really helpful in facilitating your next career steps. They may provide insight and information in your industry, have skills that would be useful for you to develop or perhaps can introduce you to people who can help you.

Identifying which people you want to build a relationship with is the first step. The following five strategic questions may help you:

1) What do you need to know that would support you in progressing your career?

2) Who has knowledge that would be useful to you?

3) Who has experience or influence in the areas you are interested in?

4) How might your existing network or contacts be connected to those people?

5) What are you able to contribute to the relationship?

Remember the importance of reciprocity to ensure a true relationship develops as opposed to using others to get ahead.

4. *Give and receive help*

Most people find it difficult to ask for help – so being the person who is prepared to take the initiative reinforces how much you value the relationship. Don't wait to be asked – use your intuition and offer help when you can see someone would benefit from your insight, experience or counsel. Being known as someone who is there for others and willingly offers a helping hand enhances your reputation. You become known as someone who cares and will put themselves out when support is needed. These are important characteristics for being a strong teammate or leader.

It is also important to be aware of your capacity; it is easy to be tempted to over commit in offering to help too many people on too many projects. When you are stretched too thin, it is likely some things will not be done well, which could undermine your professionalism, trust and rapport.

In Chapter 9, we discuss asking for help in detail because this is so often a missing skill for successful executives. Somehow, we forget that one of the most potent resources available to us is our ability to call on each other and get the help we need.

5. *Prioritise trust and safety*

Trust is a broad and complex topic, Stephen Covey[29] is often cited for his thought leadership on trust. His key message to build and sustain trust in relationships is to ensure that you clearly communicate what you are going to do and then do it. It is following through on commitments and subsequent reliability that creates trust between people. When people trust each other, we expend less energy defending our ideas and watching our back.

Trust in the workplace, and with your network requires both reliability and a sense of safety. Google, has crunched the numbers and found that the single most important factor in creating high performing teams is creating psychological safety[30].

Google's in depth analysis found it was far less important *who* you worked with – the real determinant of success was *how* you worked together. Creating an environment where it is ok to speak up and be open, without fear – and to do this in a non-judgmental and non-aggressive manner, is crucial to building relationships. In our current commercial world trust includes the ability to learn, unlearn and relearn at a rapid rate.

6. *Be curious and appreciate differences*

There will be some people who you do not have a natural rapport with and with whom building a relationship with will be more difficult. You may have had very different life experiences that make it harder to build trust and rapport. Seek to find connection with others, even though there may be a significant difference of opinion. Be curious about opposing ideas and views. You don't have to agree with them, rather, by understanding where they are coming from you are able to appreciate their perspective.

Being curious leads to asking questions that may otherwise not be considered. When you want to explore and learn from every interaction it will create a sense of connection and further develop the relationship.

Relationships are a great way to stretch our personal and professional capacity – and asking thought-provoking questions is a powerful skill. Do you really know what motivates them? Do you understand the ways in which they feel empowered? Or in what ways they feel constricted or limited?

It is interesting that sometimes the people with whom we initially have strong differences, can subsequently develop into strong relationships. Forging through a difficult situation together can bring increased respect and a shared understanding, even if there is not complete agreement.

To improve your ability to appreciate differences:

- Try letting go of the need to be right. Experiment with taking a bigger picture view and incorporating other people's perspectives

- Ask questions – seek to understand why they believe their view is the best way to move forward. Adopt an attitude of genuine curiosity

- How can you collaborate or integrate your different ideas? Sometimes what seems like an impossible situation can evolve into a better idea or outcome through collaborative thinking and integrating ideas

7. *Get to know people personally*

Relationships are deeper than being purely work colleagues. Humans truly connect when they know each other's lives and interests. Connecting with people you work with in more personal ways strengthens relationships and builds rapport and trust.

When it comes to *building* relationships, a simple *hello* can lead to a million things

Make time to have some fun together, whether it is silly celebrations, sports events, drinks, BBQs, outings or games. Having times when you can laugh and play strengthens the connection between the people you work with.

There is of course a balance; you need to understand when it is time to have fun and when it is time to dial it back and be more serious.

Building personal connections:

• Ask people about their family, interests and life beyond work

• Ensure there are regular get togethers that have plenty of time for informal conversations

• Organise some regular events and celebrations for people to participate in

8. *Get out of your own way*

Extending yourself into a broader range of relationships requires a commitment to move beyond your comfort zone. It is easy at work and industry functions to mix with the people you already know; the challenge is to make the effort to connect outside of this group. Be conscious that while it may initially feel uncomfortable, learning the skills to approach new people increases your confidence.

Be your own coach

• Consider your relationships in the workplace; who would it be worth getting to know better? How will you connect with them?

• Invest time and energy with existing relationships and regularly extend yourself to connect with new people

• If you feel nervous focus on asking questions of others – be curious and aim to learn something new in each interaction

- Research and attend groups, forums, events and networks where you have an opportunity to practice and experiment with the ideas in this chapter

- Practice actions of confidence by using informal moments, like queuing for coffee or in the lift, to have a conversation with the person next to you

NOTES

NOTES

Chapter 6

BE FOCUSED
AND PRESENT

"Living in the moment
means letting go
of the past and not
waiting for the future.
It means living your
life consciously, aware
that each moment you
breathe is a gift"

- Oprah Winfrey

In Chapter 4, Work Hard, we asked you to take part in a short attention based exercise to demonstrate the limitations of multitasking. Now, it's time to go deeper.

We are going to show you how to focus your energy and talent, become present in your day to day life and boost self awareness through your multiple intelligences – that's right, you may be surprised to find you have more than one. Each intelligence is rooted in trust and confidence, offering a wealth of insight to guide your path.

MEET YOUR INTELLIGENCES

Head/cognitive intelligence

Head/cognitive intelligence is a powerful and familiar source that, among other things, involves the ability to reason, solve problems and address complex ideas with logic and rational processes. It is so highly prized in Western culture that this intelligence is revered above all other input and sensations. Yet, if we simply stopped to take two or three deep breaths before acting or speaking, the intelligence of our heart, gut and body would become available to us. These unique systems promote productivity, awareness, connection, confidence and efficiency.

Heart/emotional intelligence

"I know in my heart that this is the way forward"

Did you know that the heart has its own nervous system? With over 40,000 neurons, it can beat without the brain and according to science is able to "independently sense, process information, make decisions and even demonstrate a type of learning and memory"[31]. Powerful, right? Yet, this hand-on-heart intelligence is often disregarded as irrational and less valuable than pure cognition.

Daniel Goleman is considered the father of emotional intelligence (known also as EQ, EI and intelligence of the heart) with his work being taught in schools, universities and businesses for over thirty years. Emotional intelligence is the ability to understand and manage your own emotions, and those of the people around you. People with a high degree of emotional intelligence know what they are feeling, what their emotions mean and how these emotions impact on other people.

EQ enables you to lead your life from the heart with awareness, compassion, kindness and vulnerability for yourself and others no matter what the challenge. When decisions need to be made, tuning into your heart is critical as it may suggest a course of action that is not immediately logical, but steeped in awareness and honesty.

Gut/intuitive intelligence

"I have this gut feeling that..."

We all have innate intuition. It often feels like a warning system that tells you it's either ok or not ok to make that decision or take that action. This radar or sixth sense communicates at a deeper level than cognitive thought; it's a primary instinct that you can't quite put your finger on but can rely on to guide your authentic direction. Again, we often ignore or override this *knowing* because we can't justify our *gut feeling.*

Intuition is what you know without seeing or touching it. You can feel the truth, even when it seems perverse, difficult or uncomfortable. Once you have accessed that truth – act from that place swiftly and decisively. You do not have to justify or explain what you know, you simply have to trust and follow the impulse.

Learning to listen to your gut intelligence takes time and is an important skill to develop. The more you do it, the stronger your intuitive self becomes.

Body/physical intelligence

"I was jumping with excitement..."

Our body responds to stimulus far faster than our minds and can be a source of valuable intel. When we feel a surge of energy or a sense of heat or cold, or sweaty palms – these are signals. Our body is letting us know it's time to pay attention – NOW! Tuning into what your body is telling you is an essential part of being able to read the environment around you.

Whenever you are in a demanding, difficult or challenging dynamic, stop and notice what your body is telling you. What are your eyes doing? Are you slouched, upright or are your feet tingling? Do you feel weak or strong, alive or deadened?

Notice also the difference between what you say and how you present yourself physically. You may be able to spot this more easily in others in the beginning.

An example might be when a team member talks about being excited about a task, but slumps in the chair with their arms folded. Motivated and inspired people tend to sit upright and lean in, they move closer to the idea being discussed. It's clear that your colleague's verbal and physical messages do not align – enabling you to ask important questions.

FOCUS AND PRESENCE

At 39, Cecile appeared to have it all: a husband with a senior role in finance, two children – one in preschool and one at primary school. At work Cecile secured and retained prestigious clients and led her team with vigour and passion. At home Cecile tried to make time for her husband and spend plenty of time with her small children.

You may be fooled into thinking Cecile was living the dream, yet scratch the surface and the chaos of keeping these balls in the air was taking a toll. Bills were unpaid, appointments were missed and many tasks were often half finished.

When Cecile started working with a coach, she learned how to focus her talent and energy, and remain present in her life. Understanding the power of these two elements decreased her sense of overload, she went from needing to be always *on* with many things unfinished, to feeling more open, less stressed and able to do more in the same amount of time.

HOW-TO:
DEVELOPING FOCUS

Focus is the ability to set priorities and move systematically from one thing to the next, completing a task in its entirety before moving on. The ability to focus puts an end to the chaos of multitasking such as criss-crossing, doubling-back, re-reading and so on.

It is easier to stay focused if we have a clear understanding of how this particular task, issue or project aligns with our values and purpose (see Chapter 1). Alignment ensures that even when there are parts of the task at hand that seem less interesting, the big picture continually reminds us of the relevance of staying with them until they are complete.

The biggest challenge to our ability to focus is *internal distraction*; the thoughts, doubts or new shiny ideas that capture our imagination and lead us off into what can seem like a more exciting or interesting place. Focus takes practice and a willingness to use all of your intelligences to persist as it is unlikely interruptions or distractions will decline in the future.

To develop the habit of focus:

1. *Find a suitable work space when periods of concentration are required*

2. *Prevent disruptions* – have a sign or email message that clearly explains when you will be available so that you are not constantly on call and reacting to the demands of others. Minimise physical distractions i.e. turn off internet access, smart-phones, emails, etc.

3. *Finish what you start* – get the highest priority task finished before starting on the next

HOW-TO:
DEVELOPING PRESENCE

To have presence requires complete attentional availability in the moment, beyond the distraction and niggles of the mind. It is quite simply *being* rather than *doing*. Presence enables you to tap into your intelligences and access your inner wisdom, unfettered by the judging and comparison that so often occupies mental processes and undermines confidence.

Practising presence for ourselves is essential to developing the capacity to be present for others. It remains a quality or a state rather than an action. With good intention, we have a tendency to go into *fix-it mode* when others are troubled, distressed or angry. Instead sometimes the most meaningful gift is the ability to sit still, listen and acknowledge what is.

Presence is quite simply *being* rather than *doing*

To build presence at work is an inner game requiring these essential ingredients:

1. **Create a solid base:** Maintain Resilience (Chapter 7), Be Authentic (Chapter 8) and Face Fear (Chapter 10) are key facets of this

2. **Remove judgement and comparison**

3. **Understand the context:** being able to sense and read the dynamic at play and clearly, calmly respond to it with authority and insight

Many cultures and wisdom traditions have known for thousands of years the unique ability of focus and presence to transform the mind. These practices are now used by working women and men throughout the world.

Becoming mindful

One of the best known ways to create focus and presence is the practise of mindfulness. Mindfulness is broadly described as the *acceptance of whatever is happening in the moment.* It is about paying conscious attention to our thoughts and feelings without reacting, judging or being swept away in thought.

Being awake to the present moment significantly reduces stress and anxiety. As a result, individuals are seeking these techniques to improve their lives and many organisations now offer a mindfulness curriculum for executives and staff. Some examples include:

• Google's Search Inside Yourself [32] program is now an acclaimed book, worldwide mindfulness course and movement that professionals can participate in

• The work of Jon Kabat-Zinn and his Mindfulness Based Stress Reduction (MBSR) [33] program has been applied within many corporations, government departments and not for profit organisations

And, why not? The benefits of mindfulness go beyond stress reduction [34]:

- An ability to be fully present, with yourself and others
- To experience difficult or unpleasant thoughts and feelings with acceptance
- To become aware of what you may be avoiding
- To become more connected to yourself, others and the world
- To be less judgemental
- To enhance self awareness
- To be less distressed and less reactive to unpleasant experiences
- To see that you are not your thoughts and feelings
- To experience more calmness and peacefulness
- To develop self acceptance and self compassion

There are many ways to achieve mindfulness – the important thing is to find a regular practice (or combination of practices) that work for you.

The mindfulness paradox

To become mindful, you must invest in yourself. Yet when life is already full, even the idea of taking a 15-minute walk or sitting for meditation practice can feel like too much. It's at these peak times that we look for relief using procrastination, bad habits or zoning out, none of which alleviate the original problem. Developing your focus and presence using mindfulness, is not another task or distraction, it is a path out of overwhelm.

HARNESS YOUR INTELLIGENCES

The fastest way to connect with your EQ, intuition and body intelligence is by becoming still, and connecting with your breathing. Stopping to take three conscious breaths interrupts the fight or flight response and minimises the *monkey chatter* of the mind.

Breathwork can take the form of a longer exercise (like meditation) or it can simply be used at various points throughout the day to focus on what needs to be done next. When you notice yourself triggered – which means wanting to react, defend, judge or argue – it is useful to take one or two minutes to stop, breathe, and find a more constructive way to express your views.

Meditation

"If it weren't for my mind, my meditation would be excellent."

- Pema Chodron

People often say "I can't meditate" or "I tried meditating and it didn't work for me". Meditation is not something that works or doesn't work. It is about intention – when the intention is to quieten the mind and let thoughts come and go, without attaching significance to them, there is no need to meditate well or perfectly.

I, (Fiona) have had a love hate relationship with meditation and breathwork. My first experience at a meditation retreat was disconcerting and uncomfortable; it seemed as though everyone else knew what to do and found it easy to sit still and breathe for an hour at a time. While for me it felt excruciatingly difficult. Over the years, having participated in many retreats, workshops and developed my own mindfulness and meditation process, I really appreciate the benefit. I've learnt that I can be mindful anywhere anytime; when I'm walking, eating, waiting for a meeting to start or feeling stressed. Once I gave up trying to get it right and relaxed into the experience a lot of the anxiety and distraction disappeared.

There are thousands of good quality mediation resources and guided meditation podcasts available online. Ask friends who meditate regularly what they use and like. Explore and experiment with different types of mediation and breathwork; find what feels most resonant for you and practice diligently.

Yoga

Yoga is an integrative practice that brings the mind, heart and body into alignment. Yoga is a regular practice of asanas (or poses) that build physical strength and flexibility through the body and breath. Many of the movements are designed to *open the heart* and to raise the level of body and intuitive intelligence available to us. Yoga also includes meditation practice and, for some people, combining their yoga and meditation practice works well. There are many different schools of yoga, try a few and find one that works for you.

Focus
on the breath

MAKE YOUR PRACTICE SUSTAINABLE

The goal is to implement a sustainable mindfulness practice that replenishes your energy, connects you with your Core Confidence and harnesses the intelligence that comes from your whole body system. On the path to focus and presence, discipline is your friend.

Be your own coach

- Create a space in your home, at work or a local park, where you can sit and just *be*

- Block out at least 15 minutes for yourself daily. Use this time for mindfulness practice, including writing your key focal areas for the day (what are you trying to achieve? Connect with your values and goals)

- Find an app that works for you: InsightTimer, Headspace, Calm are a few that you may want to try

- Write about your mindfulness experiences to solidify your practice. What are the most common thoughts arising?

- Capture how your practice helps you respond to triggers in a more resourceful way

- Use mindful techniques to become present in meetings; see if you can read the room in new ways and write down what you've learnt by observing those around you that you did not notice previously

- Apply these principles to yourself, bring a complex topic to mind and tap into what your multiple intelligences are telling you

NOTES

NOTES

BE FOCUSED AND PRESENT

Chapter 7

MAINTAIN RESILIENCE

"The best way out,
is always through"

- Robert Frost

A client, Zara, had worked for a successful not for profit (NFP) organisation for fifteen years. She had originally joined as a volunteer and had then stepped into a series of fulltime roles, earning promotions along the way. Zara strongly identified with their cause, she felt that working at this organisation was an integral part of who she was as a person and of her purpose in life. As the organisation grew, there was a major restructure during which a new board and CEO were appointed. As part of this change, Zara was informed that all the senior management roles were being re-advertised and that she would have to reapply for her role, competing against external candidates.

Zara was devastated – she felt she had given so much of herself over long years of service. She knew the organisation intimately and felt that the way the reshuffle was being managed was disrespectful to everything she had contributed. Not only was Zara unsuccessful in her application for her previous role, but as part of the restructure, Zara was made redundant. The anguish and betrayal Zara felt was like waves of deep and unrelenting grief, it felt almost as though she was abandoning her precious child. Initially she was too depressed to start searching for another role.

We worked with Zara to explore all that she had learned in her previous role and to acknowledge all that she had contributed. She spent time catching up with contacts and friends in the NFP sector.

A contract role similar to her previous position came up and she decided to accept the role while she worked out what her next steps would be. While in this role, she was asked to take a step up and fill in for the CEO when he was attending an international conference. Although some elements were familiar and relatively easy, Zara felt out of her depth at times. She realised that she would need to gain broader experience if she ever wanted to be considered for a CEO role in the future. Finally, another contract role with a different organisation came along, as their Head of Operations, and this gave Zara the opportunity to broaden her knowledge and experience.

Three years after leaving her original organisation, Zara was offered a role as the CEO for a social enterprise that combined all the skills she had gathered throughout her career.

When looking back, Zara commented, "If I had not been forced to confront that difficult ending, I would not have been available for the opportunities and new experiences that have come as a result of something that at the time felt devastating. I am now able to contribute more than I ever imagined and I'm grateful that I had to go through that challenging time".

WHAT IS RESILIENCE?

Resilience is the ability to move forward (if only millimetre by millimetre) when unexpected hardship, change or challenge arise. It is also described as the ability *to spring back into shape*. Resilient people draw on equanimity in times of adversity; they have the skill to remain calm and composed in the face of tension or stress.

Research shows that when we encounter challenging events head on, we deepen our resolve and strengthen our ability to perform. Resilience then is an invitation to go beyond the initial pain and discomfort and to embrace new opportunities.

"If we are brave enough often enough, we will fall; this is the physics of vulnerability".

- Dr. Brene Brown[35]

Brown explains that resilience is about our *tolerance for discomfort*. When you face the reality of tough emotions you are able to do tough things and work through tough situations. The old saying *what doesn't kill you, makes you stronger* turns out to be true. Brown's research examines the character traits, emotional tendencies and mental habits that enable people to transcend the difficulties of life, and emerge not only unbroken, but even more whole.[36]

We often say to clients who are experiencing hardship that "although difficult now, there is an unexpected and valuable upside to this situation and it's called *resilience*". The use of supportive strategies during these times is the fast path to mastery.

Your resilience
is what brings you
through failure

CONFLICT BUILDS RESILIENCE

Unfortunately, when it comes to human interaction, especially when the stakes are high, conflict cannot be avoided. Resilience in this context is the ability to move into difficult conversations with skill, courage, kindness and presence.

I,(Fiona) remember many times in my corporate career when the senior management team was faced with hard choices. Initially, there would be polite debate at the executive level, followed by small groups advocating for or defending their position. Sometimes these conversations were personal and involved denigrating the character of another executive. When we regrouped, the polite discussion had transformed into heated debate, sometimes shouting each other down, due to the urgency of the situation.

If we had been able to have an honest and courageous conversation upfront, decisions could have been made with less fear and emotion. Individually and collectively we did not have the resilience to lean into the discomfort of those conversations and consequentially risked both our relationships and the efficient functioning of the organisation.

It takes courage to speak up and present a different perspective. Each time you calmly and respectfully offer an alternate position, policy or solution you enhance your resilience and demonstrate the importance of being resilient to others around you.

Avoiding conflict is strongly linked to fear – it can feel unsafe to voice a different opinion to those more senior than you or stand up against something that others are passionately arguing for. Deep down you may be concerned that you will fall out of favour or feel as though you will no longer belong. In Chapter 10 *Face Fear*, we refer to the importance of *Reframing failure as feedback* to strengthen your resilience. It's important to find your voice and use it.

FOUR DIMENSIONS OF RESILIENCE

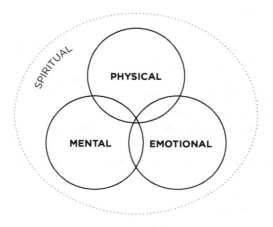

There are four dimensions of resilience pictured above. The diagram shows the physical, mental, emotional dimensions in interlocking circles, and, surrounding everything else, the spiritual dimension. These dimensions are interdependent; the more one is strengthened the more the others are reinforced.

Each dimension has specific elements that are important to focus on as you flex your resilience muscle. Underpinning the model is the need for flexibility, to move with changes and find a new way of doing things (rather than having a rigid position or overt reaction when something happens that you do not like or agree with).

It is likely that at least one (if not more than one) of the four areas is a natural strength for you. Use this as the foundation and experiment with the other areas that have not been fully utilised.

As we unpack each element, it is important to highlight that we are not personal trainers, nutritionists, psychologists or similar professional practitioners. We have, however, invested significant resources in building our personal and professional resilience across each area, over many years. Below we share the basics for building resilience in each dimension. Beyond that we encourage you to explore other resources and visit specialist practitioners if you would like tailored expertise.

Physical resilience

Move your body

Your physical health is a resilience pillar. We talk to many women who suffer ill health as a result of the demands of modern life. Physical resilience means reconnecting with your healthy body and promoting physiological wellbeing. It asks that you drop out of the thinking brain for a moment and get in touch with your physical intelligence. And, what is most encouraging about the physical dimension, is that it gives back threefold what you invest. The healthier your habits in this realm, the better decisions you make and more resilience you develop.

In previous chapters, we discussed the need for goals and focus, use these tools to create a physical activity plan that you enjoy and invite your friends along for motivation. You want to connect with – and move – your body every day.

When exercise is combined with disciplines that focus on stretching and movement such as yoga, tai-chi, qigong (which also have a spiritual and or meditative quality), you integrate building resilience across the four domains.

Physical activity is also strongly associated with good sleep patterns, and this in turn has a substantial effect on physical wellbeing. Lack of sleep, or disturbed sleep, erodes all the domains of resilience. Learn more about sleep in Chapter 4, Work Hard.

Eat for health

A big project at work is all it takes to forget everything we know about food and nutrition. If you're still slogging away at 11 o'clock at night, a packet of chips and a block of chocolate seem like a reasonable reward. The problems start when this strategy is repeated.

Humans need to eat a balance of nutrients from a variety of food groups to remain optimal. Inflammation is now thought to be responsible for much of the disease we endure and is often the result of prolonged dietary issues. Scientists are increasingly finding links between diet and wellbeing (or a lack of), including the microbiome in the gut and its association with emotional and mental states and illnesses.[37]

What food habits are inhibiting your health? Write them down to create awareness about your relationship to food in good and bad times. What changes would you like to make? What strategies could you use to prevent your unhelpful habits from taking over?

It is important to experiment and find the best path for you. There are many online resources to tap into, natural health practitioners and nutritionists to consult with and communities you can join who are also interested in improving their health through nutrition and exercise.

HOW-TO:
STRENGTHEN YOUR PHYSICAL RESILIENCE

1. *Plan and commit to your exercise and stretch or movement sessions each week*

2. *Seek out others who like similar exercise* and support each other to show up, even when you don't feel like it

3. *Learn about the foods and nutrients that are most nourishing and provide the best sources of energy* – so your body is fuelled

4. *Prepare and plan meals ahead of time* so that you are not relying on takeaway or eating packaged foods because you've got to the point of being 'hangry'

5. *Give your body a break from stimulants and inflammatory foods once or twice a year* (we detox twice a year and remove sugar, wheat and grains, dairy, alcohol and coffee during this time)

6. *If sleep is an issue for you, learn and practice sleep hygiene habits to* ensure that your body is getting the rest it needs

Mental resilience

Taking care of our mental resilience is a lifelong journey. In Australia, Beyond Blue estimates that 45% of people will experience a mental health condition in their lifetime. In any one year, around one million Australian adults have depression and over two million have anxiety.[38]

In your workplace, you may have heard of a colleague having a breakdown, perhaps this has even happened to you. In the last twelve months, more clients than ever have come to see us following this traumatic experience. Many variables contribute to a breakdown, both on a personal and professional level. What is most important is the early recognition that things feel harder than normal and to seek help immediately. Focus on implementing a self care plan and find small ways to lessen the load. The more you are aware of things that trigger a state of distress, the more skill you can develop in reducing the overwhelm and fear.

Developing mental resilience is not just about the outer edges of extreme stress, it is a skill we can cultivate in our day-to-day thoughts. Many of us have an internal voice that continually points to problems or negativity. That's right, *that* voice which reminds you of all the things you've struggled to let go of and highlights your inadequacies on cue.

Mental resilience is about meeting this voice with kindness and directing the mind to something more worthwhile or positive over and over again.

In psychology, overthinking is a common problem that can be addressed with a variety of useful interventions. In the wisdom traditions, rumination is not an issue if you're able to watch your mind with curiosity instead of buying into the story.

Finally, clarity is paramount. You want to be able to articulate what you are responsible for at any given moment in order to have a healthy level of accountability, focus, clear boundaries and the language to say "no", "not yet" or "I'm at capacity".

Mental resilience is about being able to contend with yourself and enjoying the exploration. You may also like to start building your resilience by re-reading Chapter 6 Be Focused and Present.

HOW-TO:
STRENGTHEN YOUR MENTAL RESILIENCE

1. *Be conscious of the pressure points in your life* – are you taking steps to manage these and asking for help where necessary?

2. *Be a lifelong learner* – get curious about what you don't know and when things don't work out. You are unique, which means you need to tailor strategies, tools and resources to work for you. Make it a lifelong goal to get to know your own operating procedures, so you can judge what is a good match and what is not a good match for your personal routines, strengths and limitations. Reach out for new ways and new ideas each day and adapt things to work in your world

3. *Manage your inner voice* – acknowledge the thoughts in your head and build the capacity not to buy into them

4. *Clarify the responsibility and expectation* that are consciously or unconsciously placed on you. Push back where your capacity is already full and establish healthy boundaries

5. *Let go of perfectionism and the need to be right* – when overused, these tendencies undermine mental resilience

Emotional resilience

The people who are most vulnerable to having poor emotional resilience are those who have high *emotionality* - that is, they are highly reactive and sensitive, with a poor ability to self regulate. This can be compounded by a tendency to overreact and imagine the worst case scenario when little things go wrong – sometimes called catastrophising.

The psychological term *self regulation* refers to being able to calm yourself and return to a normal state, rather than being overwhelmed by emotions, feeling anxious or as though you want to withdraw and have no contact with others. When you self regulate, you acknowledge what you're feeling and *talk yourself down* from having to act on those feelings. Recognising and dealing with your emotions will build emotional resilience.

We also talk to our clients about the skill of *emotional flexibility*. This is the ability to stay cohesive and not fragment when a difficult feeling, event or person appears. You might liken it to being centred or grounded when chaos is all around you.

Strong connections with other people, both at work and in your personal life, is an essential factor in strengthening resilience. A colleague recently moved interstate with her partner and has joined a group of girls that hike to build friendships, stay active and ultimately to create a support framework around her.

HOW-TO:
STRENGTHEN YOUR EMOTIONAL RESILIENCE

1. ***Develop greater self awareness and understanding*** of the things that soothe you and the things that cause you to overreact or catastrophise

2. ***Build your capacity to self regulate no matter what triggers you*** – this requires practice (Cognitive Behavioural Therapy or meditation can be helpful)

3. ***Be confident in your capacity to deal with what comes to you***

4. ***Be connected to others*** – maintain and invest in a strong network of supporters, friends and mentors

5. ***Create a list of small acts or experiences that fill your emotional cup.*** This may be a simple five minute break to walk the block, sit in the sun, listen to a favourite feel good song or having a quick chat with a friend who makes you laugh and smile. Like a pitstop in a car race, this allows you to refuel, refresh and last the distance

Spiritual resilience

There are two crucial aspects to spiritual resilience. The first is being clear about what you value and believe and living a life in alignment to find fulfilment and purpose. The second aspect is about how you respond when your beliefs and or values feel threatened or diminished. It is a fact of life that you will interact with people who see the world differently and do not agree with your belief structure.

Whether or not your spiritual framework is informed by a recognised faith or religion, what matters to you spiritually is critical as it forms part of the fabric of your being and is linked to your identity. Our relationship with spirituality is deeply personal. A deeper discussion is beyond the scope of this book but we feel strongly that this aspect of resilience needed to be acknowledged and included.

RESILIENCE IS REGENERATIVE

When used wisely, resilience is a tool that allows you to grieve and heal without losing your balance in the world. It promotes renewal and emergence, two very powerful human experiences that can change us for the better.

Be your own coach

- Reflecting on a recent experience where you have failed, identify how could you have used the experience to develop your resilience?

- Think about the four dimensions of resilience; which are strengths? How can you leverage these? Which do you want to spend time developing?

- Identify one or two simple self care strategies (physical, mental, emotional, spiritual) you can commit, to strengthen your resilience

NOTES

NOTES

MAINTAIN RESILIENCE

Chapter 8

BE AUTHENTIC

When you see
somebody in the
full flow of their
humanity, it's
remarkable.. *they
shine, they gleam,
they glow*

- Caroline McHugh

Simply put, authenticity is the ability to interact honestly with the world around you. It is the most powerful verbal, physical and spiritual expression of who you are in the moment. Authenticity is anything but passive, it is a quality that needs to be actively developed through deliberate and courageous self exploration.

Authenticity is also relational, describing the ever evolving relationship between your core self, your ego and the outside world. As you grow and learn, your ability to show up in the moment grows with you, whether that means leaning in or opting out (or taking action somewhere in between).

Authentic leadership is an extension of these ideas and is defined by researchers at Harvard as:

"Authentic leaders demonstrate a passion for their purpose, practice their own values consistently and lead with their hearts as well as their heads." [39]

These leaders are self aware and consciously match their words to actions, they are often regarded as present, themselves and trustworthy. Confidence and authenticity walk side by side; together they bring who you truly are into the light.

THE AUTHENTIC FEMININE

I (Fiona) recall talking to one of PWC's first female partners about her leadership experience. She told me that in the beginning she believed being a woman was a disadvantage to her progression. That was until an executive coach pointed out that she brought unique skills to the table, skills that enabled her to navigate challenging situations her male colleagues could not. In time, she realised her feminine qualities were actually a highly prized *resource*.

Everyone has both masculine and feminine traits and it is important for both sexes to own and integrate these two energetic sides of themselves.

While more women are working full-time and moving into executive roles, there remains a strong skew towards male professionals at

Safe decisions and behaviours promote the status quo. They protect us from change and discomfort, and simultaneously stifle our potential and growth senior levels. Given 70-80% of the company culture is leader led, it comes as no surprise that many organisations remain primarily masculine environments.

In the past, some women withheld traditional female traits from the workplace to avoid being seen as too emotional, too caring, not tough enough or vulnerable. It was a no win situation for everyone; organisations missed out on the innovation of feminine principles and intelligences, while female leaders were measured by the standards of the command and control leadership style of the time. Women are often caught in a double bind: condemned for their assertiveness (seen as being aggressive) or mocked for being too passive (seen as being weak).

Today, science tells us that engagement and productivity are not the natural outcomes of hierarchical, command and control structures, this is causing an evolution in leadership theory and practice. Even still, there remains a tendency for women to withhold and compromise aspects of themselves in order to fit in and 'be one of the blokes'.

I, (Fiona) recently joined a group of men on a national road-show. These were great guys who enjoyed hanging out together, drinking red wine, playing a few tricks on each other and sharing their love of many sports teams. They certainly didn't set out to exclude the women present – however, much of the conversation tended towards 'blokey' topics such as cars and sport. I was one of two women present and neither of us had much to contribute on those subjects. While it can be tempting to try to *be one of the boys* (and in some male-dominated industries that can feel the only way to be included) we need to be conscious of the cost of this approach.

To stay relevant in a volatile, uncertain, complex and ambiguous (VUCA) world, organisations are transforming to be more open, caring, innovative and collaborative. Now is the time for us to be clear and confident about how feminine traits can contribute to leader and organisational success; and to support men in accessing these strengths within themselves.

THE COURAGE TO BE SEEN

"Authenticity is a collection of choices that we have to make every day. It's about the choice to show up and be real. The choice to be honest. The choice to let our true selves be seen." [40]

- Dr. Brene Brown

As a young corporate executive I, (Fiona) was proud of my track record. I had created an expectation that no matter what was going on, I could deliver. One week everything went awry. All my planning and preparation were thrown out the window as flights were delayed, materials did not show up, a supplier was very demanding and a report needed completing. I was out of my comfort zone and even considered resigning – the idea of leaving was more bearable than being seen as less than capable.

A senior manager noticed I wasn't myself and asked if I was ok. Part of me wanted to pretend I was fine, while the other was crying out to tell the truth. I had to choose between my ego or my authentic self and I chose honesty. I admitted that I was overwhelmed to which he simply replied, "Yes, I was worried about you. How can I help?"

To be authentic we need to acknowledge that we cannot control everything and be prepared to embrace all of who we are. That means owning up to our experience, flaws and challenges and embracing our gifts and talents.

AUTHENTIC BOUNDARIES

Boundaries inform what you are prepared to accept and not accept, and what you are prepared to share and not share, in any given situation. They are defined by your values and ensure your time, energy and resources are at the service of your best self.

Much like authenticity, boundaries are relational and open to challenge and change. They influence how we see ourselves and how we are viewed by others, and are generally communicated through words, behaviour, body language and energy. They set the tone for how seriously we feel about an issue in the workplace and speak volumes about our self respect.

A healthy boundary is one that clearly establishes where your conscious limits exist at a point in time. We like this overview of the importance of boundaries from Essential Life Skills[41]

- You have a right to establish personal boundaries

- Other people's needs and feelings are not more important than your own

- Boundaries give you agency to say no

- Self trust and respect are found in boundary setting

- Keep your boundaries fresh – without questioning them from time to time, they may limit you

AUTHENTICITY IS NOT CONFESSIONAL

Part of knowing your boundaries is being clear about what is wise and appropriate to share in different contexts and situations. Revealing intimate pieces of information, for example, is rarely a good move in the workplace and can potentially undermine true connection. Further to that, some people will claim *authenticity* to justify comments that are shaming or judgemental of others; this simply reveals a lack of self mastery. There is a sweet spot between being your authentic self and not needing to burden others with unnecessary or inappropriate details or information.

Four key tools to navigate the tricky line between authenticity and oversharing:

1. *Continually deepen your self knowledge*

Commit to extending and building your self awareness and knowledge – use the exercises in this book and invest in learning that enables you to see both your strengths, and the blind spots that are getting in your way.

Comparison *corrodes* confidence

2. *Be context aware – what is the relevance?*

Check in with yourself – what is necessary and useful in this scenario? Are you oversharing to be liked? Or are you focused on the situation at hand and building rapport and trust to achieve the outcomes you require? Being too candid too early in a situation can backfire and leave people questioning your competence.

3. *Be honest*

This seems obvious however humans are often tempted to exaggerate or over-inflate their previous successes and achievements. Trust in your own experience and share your knowledge honestly, without an agenda.

4. *Do your homework*

If you are working in a different country or with an industry that is unfamiliar to you, take time to understand the cultural norms and what is shared or exchanged in that environment. This gives you the insight into what is appropriate contextually.

AUTHENTICITY PROCESS

Through our training in system dynamics, a methodology to fully appreciate the complexity and interdependence of all elements of the system, we have developed a process that enables individuals to see their patterns, uncover their deeper truth and choose a path of authenticity. It is easy to be authentic when things are going to plan and you feel in flow and unstressed. Authenticity is tested when you are in a situation that feels fearful, risky, difficult or uncomfortable.

Authenticity
is the process
of *consciously
authoring* who you
are in the world, in
the present moment

HOW-TO:
ACKNOWLEDGING YOUR TRUTH

Bring to mind an issue or situation, personal or professional that feels confronting.

5. *Notice your reaction*

The first step is to notice how you react in a situation that feels uncomfortable, risky or scary. Notice how you feel in your body – the physical sensations and the emotional feelings that arise. Take a moment to breathe and acknowledge that it is ok, and that you are going to use this information to help inform your decisions.

6. *Remember your pattern*

Once you have acknowledged your reaction, connect with the familiar pattern of what you would normally do when you feel this way. How do you normally respond? This is often conditioned by the desire to fit in or belong and can easily arise in work and family situations. Many people will recognise a flight, fight or freeze pattern – when threatened, at risk or unsafe. What happens for you?

7. *Uncover your truth*

Stage three is the most challenging, it requires you to be quiet for a moment, to dig deep, below the initial reaction and habits, and listen to what is really going on for you. This can feel uncomfortable, almost like a little niggle that you'd rather ignore. Don't ignore it any longer, let's go there and find out what is happening for you. Lean into that uncomfortable sensation and ask how could I meet this situation differently? This is the point where you can perceive and feel your authentic truth.

8. *Make a conscious choice*

Having tapped into this deeper layer of truth, you now have a choice. For you at this time, in this situation, you may feel too vulnerable or your boundaries too exposed to speak or act on your truth and that's ok.

Start experimenting with your truth in safe low risk environments, gaining the strength and experience before trialling it in areas that feel higher risk. You may realise that right now, despite some discomfort or fear, that you want to speak up, or act in accordance with that truth. We applaud your authentic self.

THE JOY OF BEING YOU

Authenticity is a quality that forces you to travel to the deepest parts of who you are and question how you want to behave, what you want to be known for and what you want to achieve.

In Caroline McHugh's 2013 TED Talk, *The art of being yourself*[42], she reminds us that there is only one you. You are given talents, opportunities and challenges to develop into who you are meant to be, and you have a relatively short amount of time to do it. With that in mind, authenticity should come easily to us but it doesn't. We constantly adapt and compromise and sometimes forgo what we really hold true. Taking time to explore and understand your truth is a vital to being in good connection with your Core Confidence.

Be your own coach

- In what ways are you prepared to be vulnerable in order to connect with your authentic self?

- What boundaries will you be aware of as you practice being authentic?

- When you notice that you are facing a challenging, difficult, scary or uncomfortable situation, what are you going to do to ensure you maintain your authenticity?

- Oversharing is not authenticity – how will you ensure you are sharing in a way that is appropriate to the context?

- How can you embrace your feminine and masculine traits to express your authenticity?

NOTES

BE AUTHENTIC

NOTES

Chapter 9

ASK FOR HELP

The Latin origin
of reciprocity is
reciprocus
which means
"moving back
and forth"

GIVE AND TAKE

There remains a cultural tendency to view asking for help as a sign of weakness, so much so that it can elicit anxiety in those doing the asking. From an early age we are taught about the importance and necessity of giving, with very few, if any, lessons in how to take. Taking has become synonymous with selfishness and so we try to avoid all association with it.

This lack of training in exchange (give and take) leads to what we call *the superwoman* syndrome. *I can do it all* goes the mantra. Super career women, super mum, super wife, friend and daughter. But, these super people, are not so super when it comes to:

• sharing the load effectively

• role modeling collaboration

• avoiding burn out and resentment

Confidence awaits you in reciprocity, the ability to give and receive in healthy doses. Asking for help is the first step.

RECIPROCITY DEFINED

Reciprocity is defined by the Cambridge dictionary as *the behavior in which two people or groups of people give each other help and advantages*. It is a word often used in the exchange of services between countries as it speaks to mutual benefit; *you scratch my back and I'll scratch yours.*

You see, when you perform **all** of the giving in a work or personal relationship, there is no actual exchange. As you haven't asked for anything, others aren't able to meet your needs by sharing their knowledge, ideas, kindness or skill for your benefit.

Unintentionally, you deny others the opportunity to give and yourself the opportunity to receive help and benefit from collaborating with others.

NO WEAKNESS TO SEE HERE

Asking for help is not a sign of weakness, in fact it might be a sign of strength. Gallup in the USA has been exploring strengths based development and leadership (www.gallupstrengthscenter.com) for the last 50 years. Their concept is easy to grasp: identify your strengths and then do more of what you're great at doing.

Through assessing our natural patterns of thinking, feeling and behaving, the online CliftonStrengths test cleverly determines what we do best and by default demonstrates how it is impossible to be super at everything. The key is to name, claim and aim the strengths you possess and leverage the talents of others in areas in which you don't have a natural interest or capacity.

I (Kate) use this principle in all facets of life. When new technology enters my home for example, I call a friend for advice. It takes me a long time to bumble my way through instructions (after I've procrastinated for a number of days), while my friend makes technological magic happen in the blink of an eye – and enjoys it. This example is simple for a reason, we can help each other in a variety of ways. Playing to your own, and others' strengths puts you in a win-win situation when asking for and offering help.

A HAPPINESS TRIFECTA

How does it feel when you help someone learn a new skill, support their project or even when you roll up your sleeves and help a friend move house? When we ask our clients these questions, they say it feels "satisfying", "worth every bit of time and effort", "amazing to watch my friend succeed and see that look of appreciation on her face".

Now, think about the last time you struggled through a situation or task. How much time, money and effort did you waste in trying to achieve the outcome on your own? If you told your colleagues or friends about it later, how many of them said "Why didn't you call me?!"

Intuitively, we know it feels good to be there for others, but science has proven that giving is a powerful tool for creating happiness and improving overall health. Dopamine, serotonin and oxytocin make up the *Happiness Trifecta*[43] when it comes to the chemistry of our body. Giving increases the production of these neurochemicals and impacts how we feel in a positive way. We owe it to ourselves and our community to implement reciprocity where possible, so that everyone has the chance to gain confidence and wellbeing through giving to someone else.

The catch is, you have to ask!

HOW-TO:
ASK FOR HELP

The ability to ask for help is a new skill for most of us to master. Start small and practice both asking for and receiving help. Observe the emotions and self talk triggered throughout this process. Being aware can help you identify and remove simple obstacles that can get in your way.

Start small

Practice asking for help with small tasks that do not require much from others. This can be done on things like getting feedback on a piece of work from a valued colleague or catching up for a quick coffee to review a project or obtain some guidance. On a personal note, try asking a friend or family member for some help with tasks around the house. Plus, there are loads of ways to ask for help in the workplace:

Could I ask your advice about..?
Could you help me with..?
I have a complex problem and need guidance, could I run it by you?
I'm inspired by what you do. Could I ask how you got to where you are over a coffee?
I've been reading about .. and don't quite understand... what do you think?
Could you show me how to..?
What is your opinion on...?
How could I improve..?

We all need help
from time to time.
Yes, even *you*

Pay attention to obstacles

When struggling with a task, take a minute or so to reflect on what the obstacles are or why things feel so hard. Think about what is required to move forward and if there is anyone who could help you achieve that progress. Consider asking for that help or even chunking it down to a specific element or step that would make asking for help a little easier.

Fair exchange

We've made the assumption that you are already well versed in giving. However, it's important to explore the concept of fair exchange. Social etiquette suggests that we repay all favours, gifts, invitations and help in the future. This feeling that we *owe* someone something is often the core psychological barrier to asking for help.

Be conscious of the invisible scorecard that may exist when asking for help and talk about it:

• What would be a fair exchange in their eyes?
• Is there anything you can offer in return?

Sometimes the process of explicitly asking these questions can extinguish the unconscious requirement to reciprocate, but, in order to achieve this you must talk about expectations. Who knows... it could lead to a wonderful collaborative relationship.

Don't be afraid of no

If the person you've asked for help is unable to be of assistance, thank them for their time and pat yourself on the back because asking *is* progress! When others provide us with a no, they role model healthy boundaries and demonstrate respect for their time. Every now and then, you may need to decline the opportunity to help as well. Learn from the people who provide a healthy no and don't give up. The old adage "I'll try anything once" needs to be replaced with "I'll try anything until I master it".

Who is on your *TEAM?*

Show authentic appreciation

Explicitly share with the giver the impact of the help. Sometimes this may be a short email, handwritten note or even a small token of appreciation, such as movie tickets. Explicitly sharing the value of someone's help, either personally or publicly, can be all the appreciation that is required.

IDENTIFY YOUR TEAM

Now you have developed a little more consciousness around your relationship with asking for help, it is time to get creative about noticing who in your network could be someone you can call on. We learned the power of your network in Chapter 5 – Build Relationships, and the positive impacts on confidence.

A great activity to complete every year is a process to identify who is on your TEAM (Together Everyone Achieves More) for the year. It's an opportunity to reconnect with your personal and professional goals and define who can help you make progress, share advice or simply provide support.

If we look at personal goals, you may consider the following people:

• Financial planners / bank advisers
• Close friends and family members
• Fitness instructors (even a friend you can train with)
• Health practitioners, i.e., naturopaths, physiotherapists, psychologists
• Intimate partners
• A coach

Turning to the professional (acknowledging many individuals will cross over into both aspects of life), you may consider:

• Team members (immediate or cross functional teams)
• Cross functional subject matter experts
• Individuals from other organisations like suppliers or clients
• Current work mates and bosses (immediate or indirect)
• Past work mates and bosses
• Senior stakeholders (sponsors - we will talk more about this)

- Close friends and family members
- Leadership coach / mentor (internal or external)
- Trainers of programs
- Thought leaders / authors of books
- Peer networks / forums

Not all of these will be one to one relationships. Sure, some will involve catching up on the phone or in person, but others may take the form of reading books, attending a free webinar or reading blog posts. The form does not matter, nor will it define the value of the relationship. What is important is the conscious proactive focus of bringing these people into your sphere of influence and the intention that is set for each relationship.

Below, we will look at three specific relationships that are often underleveraged.

Peers and colleagues

Now is an opportunity to think outside the box about those people that you interact with on a daily or weekly basis. Take a minute to reflect on the diverse strengths and skills that surround your immediate circle of influence. Extend your thoughts to other teams, stakeholders, clients or suppliers.

Some of the biggest sources of professional support in our experience have come from colleagues. Moral support through challenging times, flexibility in terms of collaborating on deadlines or help reviewing a technical question on a subject that is not your strength are just some of the opportunities available to you. All you need is the courage and good sense to start asking for help.

Mentors

A mentor is someone who gives a younger or less experienced person help and advice over a period of time. Examples can include:

- Access to an experienced source of advice and guidance
- Support with problem solving and handling challenging situations
- Opportunity to develop and improve skills and self confidence

- A non judgmental and safe place to voice challenges and frustrations
- Access to resources and networks

You may have a formal mentor or someone you would refer to as an informal mentor on your TEAM. The substance of the relationship is far more important than the form.

I, (Kate) have been very proactive in building supportive professional relationships in the form of informal mentor relationships over the past decade. Without the traditional structure of a line manager and executive team I wanted to make sure that I was surrounding myself with smart, dynamic professionals I could learn from. One year I was in New York attending a conference and ended up seated next to a fellow Australian during a morning session. With much in common (beyond our nationality) we exchanged contact details, hoping to share a coffee next time we were in the same city. That was over five years ago and we have since developed a strong friendship based on our professional interests.

Most mentors find the process of supporting or helping another person incredibly rewarding. While they are giving up their precious time, they often share how much they receive from the experience. In most situations, a good mentoring relationship is one where the mentee and mentor receive an equal amount of value from the relationship, but in different ways.

Sponsors

A sponsor is a person (normally inside your organisation) who has connections and influence (often described as a seat at the table) that can help you achieve your career goals. Sponsorship is earned through the demonstration of your good work.

Natural sponsorship develops when a senior staff member notices potential in an individual, often the same potential someone once saw in them. Increasingly organisations are implementing formal sponsor programs to help facilitate the gender balance of progression.

You can maximise a relationship with a sponsor by:

- Clarifying what you want in the context of career progression or experience. You have to be able to help your sponsor identify opportunities for you.

- Knowing your strengths and the value you bring to the role, team and organisation. A sponsor has to believe and trust the capability and potential of the individual they are advocating for (they will be risking their reputation on you).

- Show your sponsor that you are worth backing. Make sure your potential sponsor has proximity to see and hear about your strengths and capabilities. This may mean working on a project together, being involved in a meeting they chair or sharing feedback from past success.

Once trust and rapport has been built and your potential sponsor has seen, firsthand, your strengths and capabilities, ask your sponsor to help you. Sponsorship is earned over time and can help fast track career progression.

MANY HANDS MAKE LIGHT WORK

Reframing what it means to ask for help will give you the confidence to start asking your community for advice and support. Remember, we need each other to be successful both personally and professionally.

Be your own coach

Use the questions below to identify one to three areas of your life where perhaps you can leverage asking for some help:

- Reflect on a time you wanted to ask for help at work but were not brave enough to. How could you approach this differently now?

- What areas of life (personal and professional) does it feel like you are making the slowest progress?

- Looking at each area specifically – what seems to be in the way or the roadblock that is stopping you from moving forward?

- Who do you know that could help you move beyond this obstacle? Try and brainstorm two to three people so you have some options when it comes to the next step

- Get clear about how you will specifically ask for help. Make it easy for someone to know what you are seeking and how they may be able to help

- Ask

NOTES

NOTES

Chapter 10

FACE FEAR

"I have to remind myself that being afraid of things *going wrong,* isn't the way to make them go right"

- Anonymous

In high school, at the hands of a serendipitous seating arrangement, I (Kate) was introduced to three girls who would go on to become my friends for life. Together we shared the trials and tribulations of growing up and all the awful fashion choices along the way (yes, including hyper colour everything). But, despite the freedom and confidence found within these remarkable friendships, I remained sensitive to what the other kids thought of me and fretted about how to act and what to say in their company. It felt vitally important to fit in with the broader group.

My young self was on to something.

Being liked or, more aptly put, avoiding being disliked, can be a demanding endeavour that does not end at high school graduation. Our desire to belong is hardwired and impacts our social, personal and professional lives. Think about it for a moment, how many times in your career have you asked the question – What if they don't like me?

The fear of rejection is an experience we all share, but that's not where our focus is best placed. What matters most when it comes to fear is how we respond. If fact, our response could be the single most important factor in awakening Core Confidence.

WHAT IS FEAR?

Fear is an emotion designed to protect you from physical, emotional and mental danger. It sits in the most ancient part of the brain and serves an important purpose: run like crazy when a lion or wildebeest is chasing after you, fight for your life when running is not possible or stay close to the tribe and benefit from their protection. While the days of physical threats in the wild are long gone, modern life offers no shortage of regular and real threats to our mental and emotional stability.

In the corporate jungle, the greatest threat to our confidence is ourselves. Even when we have the capability and insight to lead our teams, fields and industries, we continue to use safety behaviours that look a little bit like this:

• Not applying for a new job or promotion
• Not accepting public speaking opportunities

- Not asking for a pay rise, promotion or flexibility
- Not addressing bullying behavior or conflict
- Not dealing with underperforming staff
- Not jumping at a project or work experience that would stretch our skills
- Not attending or speaking up during an important meeting

Through our experience, we have learned that decisions like these are driven by two primary safety behaviours:

1. *Over analysis*
Critiquing every thought, behaviour and decision

2. *Politeness*
Not wanting to be seen as pushy or demanding

Unfortunately, despite the many ways we attempt to justify these functions, they remain a clever distraction from what is really going on underneath: fear. The fear of getting it wrong, of looking stupid, of hurting someone, of not following the rules, of not knowing it all–ultimately, the fear of not being likable. If we can learn to recognise the fears that keep us small and lean in to the discomfort of challenging them, we will decrease their power and unleash our potential.

THE ROLE OF JUDGEMENT

Judgement is also a hardwired part of human nature. We are designed to assess (judge) our surroundings and the people we meet for safety. Neuroscientists refer to it as *in group* or *out group* judgements; where we decide if others are the same as or different from us.

To assess someone else we need something or someone to compare them to and wear a constant lens of: "How are you like me? How are you different from me?" This automatic and unconscious process both protects us from harmful people and enables us to quickly identify commonalities and build rapport. Comparison can also motivate us to try harder and do better.

But there is an unexpected outcome to this natural process that is quite unhelpful. When we use comparison to exaggerate the qualities of others and reinforce the doubts we have about ourselves, we play straight into the hands of fear and insecurity.

BREAK THE RULES

Are you a rule breaker or maker? Do you always follow the rules or are they optional?

I, (Kate) always quietly and compliantly did what I was told to do, to avoid getting into trouble and to keep other people happy. This pattern of being 'good' was etched so deeply in my psyche that I was completely unaware of it.

One day, Fiona and I were out on a walk at the top of Barrenjoey Lighthouse in Palm Beach. The track was slippery and muddy, but we persevered. When it was time to head back, I turned in the direction we had come from (down the muddy track) while Fiona started off toward a paved driveway with a big closed fence. I said to Fiona, "Where are you going? We can't go in there!" to which she replied, "Yes we can, come on".

Opening the gate felt wrong and I immediately began catastrophising: what if we get caught? What if we get in trouble? What if we get hurt? With such an onslaught of questions, it's surprising that this one never arose: "What if this isn't a big deal and I get to my car with less mud on my shoes?" (which is exactly what happened by the way).

After this experience, I became curious about how many rules I was subconsciously following out of fear. I wondered *could I move in the world with a little more freedom?* and decided it was worth finding out. So, with a racing heart, I chose to walk through the business class security gate when travelling economy and played hooky at a conference when I desperately needed some sun. It turns out that making decisions for yourself is empowering and the consequences minimal if not non existent.

Rule breaking isn't about foregoing integrity or responsibility. The purpose is to let go of old ideas about what makes you good or bad and free up the mental space to focus on what's truly important.

In a work context, this might take the form of constructively questioning processes and practices that slow down progress but are seen *as the norm*. Outside of work – on your next walk – it might mean considering the (paved) path less travelled!

To examine your relationship with rules, ask yourself:

Is it a rule or a guideline?

Is this a good rule? A right rule? A valuable rule?

Are there consequences for taking a different course of action?

Will anyone even know if I break this rule?

Are there benefits to breaking the rule?

STOP SEEKING PERMISSION

"It's better to beg for forgiveness than to ask for permission" is sound advice when it comes to progression. Sometimes the only way to get what we want, is to do it.

If you are constantly waiting for permission, you deny yourself the agency to move in a desirable direction with confidence. And, while you're waiting to be *allowed* to do something, your male colleagues may already be doing it.

A few years ago, I (Kate) was a panelist at a conference for women in media. After the session, I joined the discussion at one of the tables and sat there listening to esteemed women talk about workplace flexibility. One of the participants wanted her organisation to give the green light to flexible options. As an executive coach, I have asked countless professionals to explore what working arrangements enable them to deliver their best work, and then watched them successfully negotiate the terms with their employer.
I challenged the table with this insight and said;

"What's stopping you from creating the solution and asking for what you want? Why are you waiting for someone else to come up with the term and give you permission?"

Ask yourself the same questions about a topic that matters to you.

- What's stopping you from creating the solution and asking for what you want?

- Why are you waiting for someone else to come up with the terms and give you permission?

- Are you making decisions that benefit your future self or keeping your present self comfortable?

- Who is running *your* show?

FACING THE FEAR OF FAILURE

Clients ask us all the time: "What if I fail?" to which we respond (much to their disappointment): "You will. Maybe not now, but at some point, in some way, if you are trying new things and pushing the boundaries I can guarantee that you will fail. The question is, when this happens, what will you do?"

For most, the fear of failure is a roadblock when it comes to pursuing goals. But you have to wonder, what is failure anyway when there is so much to be gained from stuffing up, trying again and learning the lessons each experience has to teach you. Search online for *failure* and you'll end up down a rabbit hole of positive psychology articles like "Why success always starts with failure" and thousands of affirming quotes like these:

"If you learn from defeat, you haven't really lost."
- Zig Ziglar

"When we give ourselves permission to fail, we, at the same time, give ourselves permission to excel."
- Eloise Rista

"I have not failed. I've just found 10,000 ways that won't work."
- Thomas A. Edison

And, in case you needed more, you can access an entire library of TED talks designed to inspire on the topic of failure *(https://www.ted.com/topics/failure)*.

The overarching message is quite simple, getting it wrong is part of life and you must learn how to cope with its potential and inevitability.

In the early days of business, a friend and I, (Kate) were working together on marketing strategies. After a weekend seminar with an 'expert', I came home convinced that direct mail was worth a try. We crafted a long form letter, had them professionally printed, and folded them into envelopes complete with a handwritten sticky note on the front. 500 sticky notes later, we hit the streets, one letter box at a time.

These efforts resulted in a single phone call from a guy seeking dubious types of support, and my friend Emma booking one client. Some would look at this outcome and say our marketing strategy was a waste of time. We chose instead to laugh at the number of sticky notes commandeered for the exercise and focus on the fact that we were one step closer to getting it right.

When you reframe failure as *feedback*, you open yourself up to the next possibility. Throughout my career, my mentors have always reinforced that if you aren't failing, you aren't trying hard enough. It's a wonderful piece of advice for approaching situations where failure feels imminent. Finding the lessons, insights and benefits that come from not getting something right is liberating.

HOW-TO:

MAKING FRIENDS WITH FEAR

We know that fear keeps us playing a small game. The more comfortable we find ourselves, the more likely we are to stay small. It takes mental, emotional and physical energy to lean in to the discomfort and say yes to something that feels scary. But, it's worth it.

Start by reflecting on some of the things that you are fearful of?

In the workplace
E.g. Presenting to the leadership team
and looking stupid

In your personal life
E.g. Renting a flat on your own

Question your fear

Understand what is beneath the feeling of discomfort and start to challenge your concepts of safety. What, specifically, are you afraid of? Is this a legitimate physical, emotional or mental safety concern or is this about protecting you from possible feelings of rejection or pain if things should not go according to plan?

Notice fear at its early stages

The problem most people face is that they allow fear to grow in power and momentum, ignored until the feeling is so big and powerful it can become paralysing. Understand the early physical triggers that indicate when you are uncomfortable or afraid of something. Use the earliest signs to ask what is going on? You must act early to create a positive outcome. Wait too long and you will be trying to tame a tornado.

Get comfortable with change and uncertainty

The more that you put yourself in new environments, the quicker you will become familiar with the unfamiliar. By definition, if you have worked in an organisation for many years with the same or similar colleagues it will feel increasingly harder to leave that organisation and likely induce extra fear. How else can you challenge yourself?

Question the rules

As children we grow up with constant boundaries and approval seeking behavior (we learn to wait to be told if we can do something). Develop a healthy curiosity around your assumptions about the rules in your world.

Reframe failure as feedback

Failure can be an opportunity to get more information about what not to do or what you need to start doing. This helps you achieve your goals in the long run.

Prepare for failure

Develop a scenario around what you would do if going forward meant failing. What would the worst case scenario be and what would you do if you found yourself in this situation? Most people spend time worrying about *what if* scenarios without answering the specifics. The more certainty you can provide should things not go according to plan, the more comfortable you will feel.

YOUR CONFIDENT SELF

The famous American motivational speaker Zig Ziglar used to proclaim:

"FEAR has two meanings: Forget Everything And Run or Face Everything And Rise"

It's time to step into your power.

Be your own coach

When you feel the early stages of fear, try asking yourself some of these questions. They will help you face the fear and navigate towards awareness of your unconscious beliefs.

• What or who is triggering your fear? Thinking about the trigger, what is it specifically about the situation that you are afraid of?

• What would happen if your fears became true?

• If the worst happened, what options or solutions would be available to you?

• What is the best case scenario? What could you do then?

• Thinking about your professional and personal experience, what rules or beliefs are guiding your decision making?

• Who has developed or made up these rules or beliefs? Are they real rules, guidelines or beliefs?

• Are they your beliefs yours, or have you inherited them from others?

• Who do you seek permission from, in the workplace, in your personal life? What are you seeking permission for?

• Are you playing life a little too safe? What would happen if you played more courageously?

NOTES

NOTES

FACE FEAR

SECTION
THREE

"I've got this"

BECOMING AN ADVOCATE FOR CHANGE

Our intention for Core Confidence is that you use the **"How-To"** guides in each chapter to regain connection to your truly confident self; a self that can be expressed in the world in her full glory without hesitation.

As you do this, we know that many of you will be inspired to empower other women to shine brightly too. In fact, you may already be influencing those around you by stepping into your power and designing your life on your terms.

We opened the book by defining the four complex barriers affecting women in the workforce:

1. *Systemic barriers*
The subtle and long-held views that cause society to treat girls differently and structure careers and parenthood in a way that challenges women

2. *Gender bias barriers*
Those specific, well documented ways in which gender bias effectively limits career progression for women

3. *Practical barriers*
The entrenched traditional model of full-time male breadwinner is hard to disrupt when there is little support and incentive to do so

4. *Personal confidence barriers*
The way in which women consciously and unconsciously limit themselves

Now, having addressed in great depth the one area in which you have the most profound and immediate control, *Personal confidence*, it is time to open up a bigger conversation regarding the three remaining barriers: What are the dominant factors impeding the progress of women in 2018?

In this section, we will explore the latest research in each area and while some of the findings are challenging, they serve as a timely reminder about how far we have to go. We encourage you to share reflections inspired by the book with others, sparking a broader conversation, and ultimately becoming an advocate for change.

This conversation is not reserved for women alone. Both men and women have much to gain from the change ahead, and their voices are essential to breaking down these barriers.

WHAT IS ADVOCACY?

"If you believe strongly in someone or something, and feel the world at large pays too little attention, it may be up to you to change the equation"

- Ed Tessaro

The cold hard reality is that while we have made some progress, women are in the minority at the highest levels of power and decision making. In fact, based on the 2017 Global Gender Gap Report by the World Economic Forum, it will take 217 years until we close the economic gender gap[44].

In its traditional context, advocacy is about giving a voice to causes and people that struggle to be heard (groups, individuals, animals and the environment). In our context, advocacy can be both a formal and informal endeavour. We learned a long time ago that being connected to your Core Confidence is contagious. As our clients moved towards reconnecting to their authentic selves we noticed that people around them were inspired to do the same. As they asked difficult questions of their leaders, and met their internal fears with external action, others began asking "how did you do that?". It's the ripple effect and it is the outcome of living your confident self.

From our perspective, advocacy in this area is achieved by two primary leadership behaviours:

1. *Role modelling*
Unquestionable confidence in who you are demonstrated consistently and outwardly. The ability to call boundaries and enter a discussion

When you go first and embrace your *confident* self, you give permission to others to do the *same* in their worlds. You might even create a *groundswell* even without all of the knowledge or know-how. The desire to share what you learn with others.

2. *Questioning the status quo*

The ability to question organisational decisions, policies and behaviours that may limit the progression of women. The ability to ask for what you want e.g. pay or flexibility and determine what meets your needs.

As you are seen and heard in these ways, you will inevitably encounter friction. Traditional or fixed mindsets in some organisations may not be willing to immediately change their policies, ideas or behaviours, simply because you disagree or challenge them. This isn't a reason to sit back. Complicit and agreeable behaviours enable women to play well with others, but in extremes diminish effectiveness.

BEYOND PERSONAL CONFIDENCE

Let's unpack why advocacy is central to progress by taking a closer look at the multifaceted and layered societal, organisational and economic factors involved in a woman's confidence.

The inequities we are about to explore, evidenced by research, current literature and our observations of dynamics at play in the workplace, are not intended to promote an us versus them discussion. On the contrary, these findings highlight issues that impact us all. Our vision is for women and men to live their personal and professional lives beyond engrained expectations and norms.

When one gender suffers, the other cannot truly prosper.

1. *Systemic Barriers*

Childhood messages

A systemic barrier is a pattern of collective behaviour, policy or practice that disadvantages a particular group.

It starts early. Girls are socially conditioned from an early age to behave in certain ways; from the time they are toddlers, at pre-school and primary school, they are rewarded for *being quiet* and *keeping still*. It is a situation which girls have unwittingly contributed to by having a genetic developmental head start on their male counterparts. Girls demonstrate better verbal and fine motor skills and longer attention in early primary school[46]. Meanwhile allowances are made for the rambunctious or assertive behaviour in little boys.

Girls who are assertive, on the other hand, are discouraged for being too dominant or bossy. While it is unsurprising that overworked teachers are quick to praise quieter, less demanding behaviour, it does not diminish the impact of being conditioned to sit quietly to earn approval. Unfortunately, it is precisely these characteristics which will ultimately work against women when they try to compete in the workplace and behave assertively.

By the age of just six, girls are already beginning to view themselves as less intelligent than boys. In a 2016 study conducted by University of Illinois psychologist Lin Bian, boys and girls were shown four images: two of men and two of women, and asked to pick who was "really, really smart". Among 5 year olds, both boys and girls associated brilliance with their own gender, but by the age of six, only boys still held that view. It is deeply ironic and somewhat depressing that this is happening at an age when girls are outperforming boys[47].

Add to that the findings of a British Parliament inquiry in 2016, which found that girls are often either consciously or unconsciously discouraged from studying hard subjects, traditionally viewed as the preserve of males, like advanced maths, physics and computer science[48].

And it's not just in academic pursuits that girls' confidence begins to suffer. As girls become more aware of the world around them their self assurance decreases, this is largely due to the barrage of messages, across all media, that to be a revered woman requires flawless beauty, a fit, skinny body and the ability to aesthetically and sexually please men. Alarmingly, one study in the US found that by the age of six, girls had already started to express concerns about their weight or shape. By the time they had reached elementary school 40-60% of girls (ages 6-12) were concerned about their weight or about becoming too fat[49].

Given the combination of childhood messaging, and pressures of their teenage years it is hardly surprising that girls experience a significant drop in self-esteem as they progress through high school. Startling evidence conducted by the Australian Health Department[50] reveals that the system is indeed causing great distress for our girls during their high school years with concerning figures of girls self harming, suicide, anxiety and depression and a rising prevalence of eating disorders. While these issues are complex and a result of a confluence of factors; they do speak to the challenges and difficulties young women face as they grow up in our society, ultimately impacting their relationship with confidence.

Adult assumptions

The systemic barriers continue once women join the workforce. After a certain age it is assumed that women will want to have children. Those who choose not to, are viewed harshly by society as subverting the expected female role of nurturing mother; however, those who do choose to have a family are inevitably forced, consciously or unconsciously, to make a decision about priorities when it comes to family and work.

Women are still seen as the primary care givers, and therefore it is assumed that they will take a disproportionate role in looking after young children (and often older parents – increasingly at the same time). The assumption quite widely held by society that women are, and should be, happy to give up their financial security and future to become the primary carers of children is unfair. When women do pursue a career there is societal pressure of *mother guilt* - the assumption that children miss out on something if their mother is at work more than she is at home. This same assumption is not applied when fathers are absent from their children due to his work related commitments. These double standards are inextricably linked to creating a situation where women often feel they are damned whatever they do.

2. *Gender Bias barrier*

Strongly connected to the systemic factors that impede women's progress at the highest levels of power, are the biases we hold

The *confidence gap* starts young; between elementary school and high school, girls' self-esteem drops *3.5 times* more than boys[45]

individually and collectively – both conscious and unconscious. Bias means that we favour a particular view or outcome because it matches our internal references and frameworks – it feels aligned to what we *know* is true. Some bias is useful in decision making, however unexamined or unknown bias can have a profoundly negative impact on whole groups in society.

To illustrate the prevalence of bias in the workplace, we have included some examples that are often so subtlety part of our culture, we hardly see them:

'She is not tough enough" or "She's too aggressive"

There is a bias that leaders are supposed to possess a masculine leadership style, yet while these behaviours in men are seen as commercial, they are often viewed as aggressive in women. Similarly, considerate behaviour in men is seen as rounded and emotionally intelligent while in women as weak or soft. Research by Stanford University's Clayman Institute for Gender Research found that men are significantly more likely to critique females for coming on too strong. The study found that women received 2.5 times the amount of feedback men did about aggressive communication styles, with phrases such as "your speaking style is off-putting"[51].

"He's a great cultural fit for the team"

The job and who fills it is affected by our tendency to promote and select people who are like us. Without realising they are doing it, male senior leaders are more likely to hire other males because that person is similar to them and is perceived to be a better *team fit*.

In 2012 Jo Handelsman with Corinne Moss-Racusin at Yale University conducted an experiment as part of her research into gender bias in STEM facilities. She asked one hundred biologists, chemists, and physicists at academic institutions to evaluate identical resumes of a candidate named either "Jennifer" or "John." Despite having identical qualifications and experience as John, Jennifer was perceived as significantly less competent. As a result, Jennifer experienced a number of disadvantages that would have hindered her career advancement if she were a real applicant. Because they perceived the

LOADED LANGUAGE

A study of performance reviews has found that, compared with men, women receive:

2.5 TIMES
as much feedback about having an aggressive communication style

---

2.4 TIMES
as many references to team accomplishments

ABOUT HALF
as many references to their having vision

ABOUT HALF
as many references to their technical expertise

ONE-THIRD
as much feedback linked to a business outcome

Source: Stanford University, Clayman Institute for Gender Research
THE WALL STREET JOURNAL

female candidate as less competent, the scientists in the study were less willing to mentor Jennifer or to hire her as a lab manager. They also recommended paying her a lower salary. Jennifer was offered, on average 13% less than John[52].

The point is, given the bias, Jennifer wouldn't have been chosen for the role in the first place.

"Martin always has such great ideas; why doesn't Maria contribute more?" *(despite Maria mentioning the same thing 10 minutes earlier!)*

We hear and listen to men more than we hear women. In meetings, in conference and video link-ups, even in the elevator – we listen and recognise what men have said. When a woman raises an issue or presents an idea, it is often overlooked or appropriated by a man. This is compounded by the fact that men and women interrupt when a woman is speaking far more than when a man speaking[53].

Other examples of gender bias we have observed in the workplace include:

- Women are often expected to do the *office housework* duties that are not part of their job description such as taking notes in meetings, planning parties, clearing up afterwards etc.

- Women are more likely to be asked to serve on committees and contribute to non-work specific aspects of departmental and workplace life

- Women are often judged for their appearance (behind closed doors) – on their clothing, weight, attractiveness, etc., whereas men are rarely judged in relation to their appearance

- Men are more likely to develop sponsor like relationships with high performing males than they are with younger women because both parties may not want to be seen to favour a young woman in that way, in case it is misconstrued

Which brings us to the gender pay gap

As the Jennifer/John experiment showed, gender bias is one of the reasons why women continue to be paid less than their male counterparts and it's not because there is a lack of awareness. Every week the subject comes up on talk shows, in the newspapers, online media, acceptance speeches at awards ceremonies, it goes on and on.

Let's look at the data:

• The full-time average weekly ordinary earnings[54] for women are 15.3% less than for men[55].

• Among non-public sector organisations with 100 or more employees, the gender pay gap for full-time annualised base salary is 17.3%, and for full-time annualised total remuneration is 22.4%[56].

• Average superannuation balances for women at retirement (age 60-64) are 42.0% less than those for men[57].

Women on boards

Against this fairly gloomy backdrop of gender bias and pay gaps, there appears to be a small beacon of light. The number of women on boards is held up as a continuing success story as we move towards diversity outcomes. Women hold 13.7% of chair positions, 24.9% of directorships, as well as represent 16.5% of CEOs and 29.7% of key management personnel in Agency reporting organisations[58].

The Australian Institute of Company Directors AICD 2017-18 quarterly Gender Diversity Progress Report reported female representation of 26.7%[59] on the ASX 200 Boards (an increase from 8.7% in 2006)[60]. Interestingly, it went on to note "the barrier to achieving gender diversity on boards continues to be not one of supply, but rather of demand with an insufficient number of boards perceiving gender diversity as a strategic imperative." While women are slowly increasing representation at board level, some boards remain unaware of the business case for ensuring women have a voice at the table.

Why will a 25 year old woman entering the workforce today have lifetime earnings of one million dollars less than a man with equivalent education and skills. Why does the earnings gap increase with education? Why will a 25 year old woman with a postgraduate degree entering the workforce this year [2012] earn $1.3 million less than a 25 year old man with equivalent education? Why are there so few women leading our companies?

- Anne Summers author of
'The Misogyny Factor'

3. *Practical barriers*

Permission to have it all

As we have already seen, society has placed particular expectations on women's shoulders: the expectation that they will look good (be slim, stylish and healthy), that they will step up as nurturers and carers (whether it be for children, aging parents or other family members) and that they will also, like their male counterparts, set aside time for professional and network development. The trouble is, in an age when long working hours is still seen as a pre requisite for corporate success, when do you fit it all in?

With so many demands and so much pressure, women can feel that they are left with little choice. The leaky pipe is how many refer to this trend of women who opt out of a traditional corporate career in favour of a more flexible opportunity such as consulting, working for smaller organisations and start ups or even establishing their own small business. In fact, one third of all small business owners are female[61] and, based on conversations we've had in our network, this trend is likely to grow.

The truth is pursuing career success in corporate Australia and at the same time prioritising other areas of life is hard for women and men. Many of the role models held up for shattering the glass ceiling have made substantial compromises at a personal level to achieve their success. Few are juggling the pressures of family, financial, and personal demands that characterise the lives of average working women.

Women have permission to *have it all* but for most the reality of having it *all at once* is the challenge. When you get clear about what you want, what is most important to you (what you value) you have the opportunity to make a choice about what is important to you today and yes *you can have that all*. Over time, 12 months or perhaps 3 years you can achieve everything you want, just not all in one day.

Flexibility

Some would point to the rise in flexible working practices as the answer to these pressures. Most organisations are now on board with providing more autonomy as to where and when employees can work with 68.3% of organisations reported to have a policy and/or strategy for flexible working[62]. This flexibility impacting both males and females has eased some of the traditional friction felt by those juggling work, family, home and personal commitments. We are hearing many stories describing the freedom this new way of working has afforded.

However, there is a flipside to the rise in flexibility: organisations expect in return that employees be available almost 24 hours a day, 7 days a week, mirroring customer demands driven by technology and globalisation. This trade-off can make it feel as though there is a high price to the benefits offered from flexibility.

FLEXIBILITY CAN BE A WIN/WIN

One client, a full time working mother of two boys asked to work from home one day a week so that she could be a little more effective and also be home one afternoon a week to participate in after school activities. The impact this change had on her personal and professional wellbeing was almost unbelievable. Not only was she able to fulfil some of the commitments she was wanting to do in her role as a mum, she felt like she was able to be more productive away from the workplace where meetings, team mates and phone calls can sometimes limit the level of work that can be completed, a sentiment shared by most who enjoy this level of flexibility.

Part-time = part commitment

Over the past decade the definition of a part-time worker has expanded both in profession and nature. As the necessity to embrace workplace flexibility has become essential, part-time roles have expanded beyond the two or three days a week and beyond working mothers. Single professionals wanting to pursue alternate career passions, working fathers looking to achieve a more balanced life or baby boomers heading towards the twilight of their career are looking to stay in the workforce and make a contribution. There is however still a widespread perception that part-time work equals part-time commitment and the reality for most is that this is a hand brake on career progression.

To combat this mentality we have seen the emergence of the four day work week which, in our ever-connected, accessible and available world, often equates to full-time employment dressed up as flexible working opportunities with a 20% pay cut.

The sad reality is that moving to a part-time basis is seen as a *lifestyle choice* and there is an attitude by some companies that any exclusion these workers may feel from corporate life and culture is of their own making and not something the organisation needs to be responsible for. This can be a bitter pill to swallow when compared to the lengths that companies go to make a remote worker in rural areas feel part of the team.

Managing the home

While a growing number of men are more involved in domestic duties, women still do a far greater proportion of this work.

Australian Bureau of Statistics data from the 2016 Census shows that women spent nearly twice as long as men on primary activities associated with unpaid work. Women were also likely to spend more time on domestic activities (2 hours 52 minutes per day compared with 1 hour and 37 minutes per day for men)[63]. This emotional labour is often unrecognised in evaluating the contribution to a functioning household, yet it is essential to all members of the family and the broader society.

Parenting

It's hard to believe now, but in the 1960s women had to resign from the Australian Public Service once they got married. Far behind us now, most would say that society has accepted and embraced working married women and mothers. Either by choice or financial necessity, many women are returning to work after having children, yet pursuing career success at all levels requires compromise.

The *obligation* that evolves for working mothers, in particular, is a very precise one; the feeling that one ought to work as if one *did not* have children, while raising one's children as if one *did not* have a job

- Annabel Crabb,

The Wife Drought[64]

Financial compromise

Some parents end up spending over $150 a day for childcare or $250 a day for a nanny should the drop off, pick up tirade become too challenging. Or, for those choosing to work part-time or in casual employment, the cost is in the reduced salary and superannuation that they then miss out on.

Relationship compromise

The weight of work, parenting and career can take its toll with little space left for the primary relationship with your partner. Once on a corporate path, women often find that quality time with their children is also compromised.

Career compromise

You can end up compromising on your career – as the weight of juggling a million balls makes it too hard to *do it all.*

Parental Leave

Australia and the US have been slow to embrace sufficient paid parental leave and this has a big impact on how we can take care of our children and earn sufficient income.

- Since January 2011 Australian mothers and fathers have had access to government funded paid parental leave. The scheme provides eligible working parents with 18 weeks Parental Leave Pay at the National Minimum Wage, and can be shared between both parents.
- On 1 January 2013, the Paid Parental Leave scheme was expanded to include a new two week payment for working dads or partners.
- Fewer than half of employers offer paid parental leave in addition to the government scheme[65].

Other countries have decided to take major steps to address these practical barriers – however this is usually only done when there is widespread acknowledgement of the systemic and bias barriers.

Norway is one such country:

• Maternity leave is legislated at 100% of women's salary for 49 weeks[66]
• Norway was also the first country to introduce a fathers quota in 1993 that reserved a part of the year-long paid parental leave for dads - currently 10 weeks[67]
• Men are expected to take advantage of this leave and it is frowned upon if they do not. As a result, 9 out of 10 fathers share parental leave, up from about 2% 20 years ago, enabling women to go back to work sooner[68]
• The country's extensive system of child care, guarantees a place for 1-year-olds and after school and vacation care, and statutory paid leave to stay at home with sick children. This facilitates the 76% of Norwegian women, and 83% of mothers with small children, to work outside the home[69]
• Parents also have the right to work part-time until their youngest child turns 10[70]

Impressive right? Norway was also the first country to impose a female quota for board directors in about 400 publicly listed and state owned companies, lifting the share of women to 40%, from about 7% in 2003[71].

A number of other countries have recently imported some of the same social engineering undertaken in Norway: Germany has allocated two of their 14 months paid parental leave for fathers. As a result, the share of men taking time off with baby has swelled to 35.7% in 2015 from 3.5% in 2007[72].

IN SUMMARY

Our whole societal infrastructure has a systemic bias towards women earning less and being in the home and men working more, being in higher paid more prestigious jobs and having far less responsibility in the home.

We like to be optimistic about our progress but, as uncomfortable as it is, we need to accept that we have constructed a world where it is difficult for women to rise to the highest positions of power and equally participate in decision making. The challenge for organisations (and both the men and women within them) is to acknowledge that discomfort, accept the need for change and undertake the steps necessary to address the barriers currently costing society, and the individuals within it, so much. And this is where advocacy comes in.

HOW-TO:
ADVOCATE

So, what can you actually **do** at an individual level to make your mark and chip away at the barriers that may limit you and others?

- **Open-up dialogue**
  What statistics standout most to you? Discuss them with friends. Introduce the topic by simply asking *Did you know...?*

- **Role model for others**
  Be a living example. Feel the fear and, with self kindness, have a go! Practise speaking up and being seen, challenge yourself to call boundaries that demonstrate the respect you have for yourself and expect from others.

- **Pay your lessons forward**
  Once you're on the Core Confidence journey, you are likely to learn a lot about how the dynamics are playing out. As you uncover the insights this path leads to, share them with your network. If a mentor provides sage advice, share it with others when needed.

- **Ask the hard questions**
  If you recognise bias, challenge organisational and leadership thinking when it is appropriate to do so. Bias is often unconscious, so enter the discussion without judgement...yet armed with knowledge. It is said that we cannot un see what we have seen. By pointing out bias at play, you might change someone's perspective for life.

- **Start a network within your organisation**
  Use your advocacy to build relationships and bring women together. This can be a formal or informal gathering. Ask your network to suggest speakers (or have a go at speaking yourself) to help women think differently and grow.

Whether it is a micro step or a big leap, start where you are most passionate. When a critical mass of women embody and share their confidence with the world, we can have a systemic and game changing effect.

Catherine Fox, in her book Stop Fixing Women[73] eloquently unpacks many of the entrenched biases women face in the workplace. (For those who want to read more about these barriers and biases, we highly recommend this book). Catherine provides excellent advice for men and women who recognise the importance of shifting the current dynamic:

"When you are confronted by or see biased, sexist or dismissive behaviour or comments respond calmly with either "What did you mean by that?" or "Would you please repeat that?". These simple, non aggressive interventions highlight old patterns that are no longer acceptable".

IT'S JUST THE BEGINNING

"For decades, women have misunderstood an important law of the professional jungle. It's not enough to keep one's head down and plug away, checking items off a list. Having talent isn't merely about being competent; confidence is a part of that talent. You have to have it to excel"

- Katty Kay and Claire Shipman, The Confidence Code

When we began writing Core Confidence in 2016 we were determined to answer the following questions:

Why don't some women negotiate pay rises?

Why don't some women set boundaries?

Why don't some women speak up on important issues?

Why don't some women put themselves forward for bigger roles?

Why don't some women create flexible options and demand them?

Why don't some women give themselves permission to have it all, on their terms?

Simply...

A lack of confidence.

As we read the research and worked with our clients who began implementing the concepts and strategies discussed in Section 2 of this book, it became clear that there are many complex dynamics at play when it comes to the confidence conversation (as discussed above in Section 3). While these can be influenced over time the one area where you can have complete control and the most powerful potential to change your experience is exploring and reconnecting with your Core Confidence.

That realisation led us to this book.

We want you to experience the feeling of *I've got this* and be able to withstand the judgement and challenge of being true to your authentic and most powerful self. When you own your brilliance, there isn't anything you can't do.

Never underestimate the impact of the choice, voice or acts you do; while seemingly small they can have a big impact on you, your future and the system.

Remember

The act of confidence comes before the feeling of confidence

Now it's your turn...

ACKNOWLEDGEMENTS

This book and our work in *Core Confidence* found us. We became fascinated about this topic through conversations with friends and clients, as we realised this elusive subject of confidence was having a big effect on the careers of women. We heard women say they were often told that they needed more confidence to advance their careers, with little specific information on what that would look like. At the same time, seemingly confident women who had achieved a lot in both their career and life told us that actually underneath it all they often felt a lack of confidence. What started as curiosity and research, evolved into the model we share in the book and a deeper investigation of the barriers that impact confidence. We are enormously grateful for the support and encouragement we have received from family, friends and colleagues. In particular we are grateful to Jules Stopp; your editing skills, ideas and sense of narrative have greatly enhanced the work. We also want to thank our wonderful pre-readers, Heidi Todd, Nicole Dennis, Kristine Vergara, Jill Morrison, Louise Mace, Rosemary Pearman, Christina Roren, Sammi Jaeger and Sue Snabb for providing a fresh perspective, insights and suggestions. Finally, to the women and girls that hold the future of work in your hands and hearts, we trust that this book will support you to courageously step into a strong (re)connection with your Core Confidence.

NOTES

Section One: The Illusion Delusion

1. Adapted from Dr Russ Harris, author of The Confidence Gap

2. Workplace Gender Equality Agency, "Australia's Gender Equality Scorecard: Key Findings from the Workplace Gender Equality Agency 2015–16

3. Workplace Gender Equality Agency, "Australia's Gender Equality Scorecard: Key Findings from the Workplace Gender Equality Agency 2016–17

4. Chief Executive Women, ASX200 Senior Executive Census 2017

5. Australia's gender pay gap statistics (PDF) Australian Government. February 2018 https://www.wgea.gov.au/addressing-pay-equity/what-gender-pay-gap

6. World Economic Forum, The Global Gender Gap Report 2017

7. Australian Institute of Family Studies, Parents working out work, Jennifer Baxter, Australian Family Trends No. 1 — April 2013 https://aifs.gov.au/publications/parents-working-out-work

8. Australia's gender equality scorecard, Workplace Gender Equality Agency November 2017

9. Institute of Leadership & Management, Ambition and gender at work February 2011

10. Columbia Business School, Press release November 28, 2011 Men's Honest Overconfidence May Lead to Male Domination in the C-Suite

11. BYU News, Study: Deciding by consensus can compensate for group gender imbalances, September 17, 2012 | Joe Hadfield

12. "It Had to Be You (Not Me!) Women's Atributional Rationalization of Their Contribution to Successful Joint Work Outcomes, Michelle C. Haynes and Madeline E. Heilman, Personality and Social Psychology Bulletin 2013

13. The Myth of the Ideal Worker Does Doing All the Right Things Really Get Women Ahead, Catalyst 2011, Nancy M. Carter & Christine Silva

14. Women Don't Ask: The High Cost of Avoiding Negotiation - and Positive Strategies for Change - February 27, 2007 by Linda Babcock & Sara Laschever

15. Advancing Women in Australia: Eliminating Bias In Feedback and Promotions, Bain & Company & CEW Advancing-Women-in-Australia, March 2017

Section Two: Core Confidence - The Building Blocks

Chapter 2: Set Goals and Take Action

17. Research by Dominican University of California psychology professor Dr. Gail Matthews found that more than 70 percent of the participants who sent weekly updates to a friend reported successful goal achievement (completely accomplished their goal or were more than half way there), compared to 35 percent of those who kept their goals to themselves, without writing them down. https://www.dominican.edu/dominicannews/study-highlights-strategies-for-achieving-goals

Chapter 3: Know Your Stuff

18. Reshma Saujani, Teach Girls Bravery Not Perfection, TED Talks https://www.ted.com/talks/reshma_saujani_teach_girls_bravery_not_perfection

19. World Economic Forum, Future of Jobs 2016

20. Carol Dweck, Mindset: The new psychology of success

Chapter 4: Work Hard

21. Boston University, Research, Sara Rimmer, (Draw from Erin Reid's Study on 80 hour work week, published in Organizational Science, Embracing Passing, Revealing, and the Ideal Worker Image: How

People Navigate Expected and Experienced Professional Identities (https://www.bu.edu/research/articles/erin-reid-80-hour-work-week/)

22. The Research Is Clear: Long Hours Backfire for People and for Companies, Sarah Green Carmichael AUGUST 19, 2015 (https://hbr.org/2015/08/the-research-is-clear-long-hours-backfire-for-people-and-for-companies)

23. Daring Greatly: How the Courage to Be Vulnerable Transforms the Way We Live, Love, Parent, and Lead by Brené Brown

24. Stephen Covey, The 7 Habits of Highly Effective People

25. Brandon Rigoni, Jim Asplund, Developing Employees' Strengths Boosts Sales, Profit and Engagement, Harvard Business Review, September 01, 2016

26. Workplace Productivity, Distraction is the Nemesis of Productivity, Kate Boorer & Dr Lucia Kelleher 2013

27. Stephen Covey, The 7 Habits of Highly Effective People

28. Tom Stafford, How sleep makes your mind more creative, 2013

Chapter 5: Build Relationships

29. Stephen Covey, The 7 Habits of Highly Effective People

30. Julia Rozovsky, analyst, Google People Operations November 17, 2015, The five keys to a successful Google team (https://rework.withgoogle.com/blog/five-keys-to-a-successful-google-team/)

Chapter 6: Be Focused and Present

31. The Intelligent Heart, from Quantum Training Institute Website

32. Search Inside Yourself Leadership Institute (siyli.org)

33. Jon Kabat- Zinn, Guided Mindfulness Meditation https://www.mindfulnesscds.com/

34. Benefits adapted from Dr Russ Harris (https://www.actmindfully.com.au/about-mindfulness/)

Chapter 7: Maintain Resilience

35. Brene Brown, Rising Strong

36. 3 Quarks Daily Blog, Review of Brene Brown's Rising Strong

37. Giulia Enders Gut: the inside story of the body's most under-rated organ

38. Beyond Blue Website – The Facts (beyondblue.org.au)

Chapter 8: Be Authentic

39. Bill George, Authentic Leadership, Harvard business Review, May 17, 2007 https://hbr.org/ideacast/2007/05/harvard-business-ideacast-43-a.html

40. Brene Brown, The Gifts of Imperfection: Let Go of Who You Think You're Supposed to Be and Embrace Who You Are

41. Z Hereford, Healthy Personal Boundaries & How to Establish Them https://www.essentiallifeskills.net/personalboundaries.html

42. Carolyn McHugh, The art of being yourself, TEdxMiltonKeynesWomen

Chapter 9: Ask for Help

43. Eva Ritvo M.D, Psychology Today Apr 24 , 2014 https://www.psychologytoday.com/us/blog/vitality/201404/the-neuroscience-giving

Section 3: Becoming an Advocate for Change

44. World Economic Forum, The Global Gender Gap Report 2017

45. American Association of University Women, Shortchanging Girls, Shortchanging America (1991), http://www.aauw.org/files/2013/02/shortchanging-girls-shortchanging-america-executive-summary.

pdf. Page 7 Graph B, Self Esteem Index

46. Sally Goddard Blythe, MSc, Consultant in Neuro-Developmental Education, 2016, http://sallygoddardblythe.co.uk/boys-twice-likely-fall-behind-girls-early-years/.

47. Gender stereotypes about intellectual ability emerge early and influence children's interests: Lin Bian, Sarah-Jane Leslie, Andrei Cimpian, January 2017 Science 355,389–391 (2017

48. British Science Association http://data.parliament.uk/writtenevidence/committeeevidence.svc/evidencedocument/science-and-technology-committee/closing-the-stem-skills-gap/written/48437.html

49. Body Image, Second Edition, A Handbook of Science, Practice, and Prevention. Edited by Thomas F. Cash and Linda Smolak 2011

50. The Mental Health of Children and Adolescents. Report on the second Australian Child and Adolescent Survey of Mental Health and Wellbeing, August 2015 Department of Health, Canberra, Australia.

51. Shelley Correll and Caroline Simard, Stanford University, Clayman Institute for Gender Research, April 2016

52. Corinne A. Moss-Racusin, John F. Dovidio, Victoria L. Brescoll, Mark J. Graham, and Jo Handelsman PNAS 9 October, 2012. 109 (41) 16474-16479

53. Influence of Communication Partner's Gender on Language Adrienne B. Hancock, Benjamin A. Rubin. First Published May 11, 2014

54. Ordinary time earnings used comprise regular wages and salaries in cash, excluding amounts salary sacrificed. For more information refer to: http://www.abs.gov.au/ausstats/abs@.nsf/mf/6302.0

55. WGEA (2017), Gender workplace statistics at a glance February 2018 WGEA Data Explorer, data.wgea.gov.au

56. WGEA (2017),Gender workplace statistics at a glance February 2018 WGEA Data Explorer, data.wgea.gov.au

57. Clare R. (2017), Superannuation account balances by age and gender, December 2017, ASFA Research and Resources Centre

58. WGEA (2017),Gender workplace statistics at a glance February 2018 WGEA Data Explorer, data.wgea.gov.au

59. AICD, The December 2017 – February 2018 quarterly Gender Diversity Progress Report

60. 2006 EOWA Australian Census of Women in Leadership

61. 2071.0 - Census of Population and Housing: Reflecting Australia - Stories from the Census, 2016 LATEST ISSUE Released 27/03/2018 In 2006, 31% of all business owner managers in Australia were female and 69% male. A decade forward, and 33% were female and 67% male.

62. WGEA Australia's gender equality scorecard November 2017

63. ABS, Work and Family Balance, 2016 http://www.abs.gov.au/ausstats/abs@.nsf/Lookup/by%20Subject/4125.0~Feb%202016~Main%20Features~Work%20and%20Family%20Balance~3411

64. Annabel Crabb, The Wife Drought: Why women need wives and men need lives

65. WGEA Australia's gender equality scorecard November 2017

66. The Norwegian Labour and Welfare Administration (NAV), Arbeids- ogvelferdsetaten 2018

67. Fathers on Leave Alone in Norway: Changes and Continuities, Elin Kvande and Berit Brandth, December 2016

68. Fathers on Leave Alone in Norway: Changes and Continuities, Elin Kvande and Berit Brandth

69. Early Childhood Education And Care Policy Review Norway: Arno Engel, W. Steven Barnett, Yvonne Anders and Miho Taguma, 2014

70. Brandth, B., Kvande, E (2017) Norway country note www.leavenetwork.org/fileadmin/Leavenetwork/Country_notes/2017Norway_2017_FINAL.pdf

71. Women on Board for Change: The Norway Model of Boardroom Quotas As a Tool For Progress in the United States and Canada, Anne Sweigart 2012 Northwestern Journal of International Law and Business

72. Fathers in Charge? Parental Leave Policies for Fathers in Europe, Clara Albrecht, Anita Fichtl and Peter Redler, ifo DICE Report 1 / 2017 March

73. Catherine Fox, Stop Fixing Women, 2017